So Sweet!

So Sweet!

Cookies, Cupcakes, Whoopie Pies, and More

Sur La Table

**Andrews McMeel
Publishing, LLC**

Kansas City • Sydney • London

Andrews McMeel Publishing, LLC
an Andrews McMeel Universal company
1130 Walnut Street, Kansas City, Missouri 64106

www.andrewsmcmeel.com

11 12 13 14 15 WKT 10 9 8 7 6 5 4 3 2 1

ISBN: 978-1-4494-0728-5

Library of Congress Control Number: 2011921504

Recipes adapted from *The Art and Soul of Baking* and *Baking Kids Love*

Photography
Maren Caruso: p. vi, 2, 5, 11, 13, 14, 19, 22, 29, 33, 37, 42;
Ben Pieper: p. ii, 39, 50, 59, 72, 85, 88, 93, 96, 99, 104, 106, 117, 118, 120, 130;
JohnsonRauhoff: p. 7, 26, 47, 56, 63, 65, 69, 79, 113, 125

Design: Holly Ogden

www.surlatable.com

••••••••••••••••••••••••••••••••••••••

ATTENTION: SCHOOLS AND BUSINESSES
Andrews McMeel books are available at quantity discounts with bulk purchase for educational, business, or sales promotional use. For information, please e-mail the Andrews McMeel Publishing Special Sales Department: specialsales@amuniversal.com

Introduction

There's no denying it. Life is challenging and some days are more difficult than others. But sometimes a homemade sweet and a glass of milk are all it takes to remind us that life does have sweeter moments. Even if you're all grown up and prefer your sweets with a cup of coffee or tea, you're certain to find something reminiscent of a childhood favorite in this tasty little book.

Baked doughnuts offer a healthier option to traditionally deep fat–fried ones. No need to wake up at the crack of dawn to produce the simple doughnut recipes we offer. However, as the enticing aromas of Nutmeg Puff Doughnuts or Maple and Bacon Doughnuts waft through the house, you just may find that everyone else is up and out of bed earlier than usual.

Bakers' continued fascination with cupcakes guarantees their place among baked treats as being more than just a fad. You'll find an entire chapter offering some unique variations that are certain to keep cupcakes a popular sweet in your home for years to come.

Few people can resist homemade cookies and the variety seems endless. In this little book we've narrowed the recipes to more than a baker's dozen we think will satisfy any sweet tooth.

Debates about whether whoopie pies are of Amish origin or an East Coast secret won't matter after your first, sweet bite of Gingerbread Whoopie Pies with Orange Buttercream Filling. But we can almost guarantee that everyone will be smiling when you bake and share "whoopies" with friends and family.

Despite life's ups and downs, with these recipes and a little time in the kitchen, life can still be oh so sweet.

Cookies

Ingredients

Cookies

1 cup (2 sticks) unsalted butter, softened

¾ cup sugar

1 large egg, at room temperature

2 teaspoons pure vanilla extract

2¼ cups unbleached all-purpose flour

¼ teaspoon salt

Icing

3 cups powdered sugar

¼ cup meringue powder

½ cup water

Food coloring, in various colors to decorate

Sprinkles, sugar pearls, large crystal sugar, dragées, and/or candies

Be Creative

Sugar Cookies

MAKES 25 TO 30 FUN SHAPES

Here's a deliciously crisp and tender sugar cookie that can assume many shapes and be served as is, or sandwiched with jam, chocolate, or your favorite filling. The cookies also make a great canvas for decorating at holiday times. Use colored icing, decorating sugars, or sprinkles in your own special style.

1   Position 1 oven rack in the top third of the oven and 1 oven rack in the bottom third of the oven, and preheat the oven to 350°F. Line 2 baking sheets with parchment paper.

2   Make the cookies. Put the butter and sugar in a large bowl. Using a mixer, beat on low speed for 1 minute. Turn up the speed to medium and beat for another minute. The mixture should be blended and smooth. Turn off the mixer. Using a silicone spatula, scrape down the sides of the bowl. Add the egg and vanilla and beat on medium-low speed until well blended. Turn off the mixer. Scrape down the sides of the bowl.

3   Put the flour and salt into a medium bowl and whisk until blended. Add the dry ingredients to the butter mixture and beat on low speed just until the ingredients are blended and no patches of flour are visible. The mixture will have the texture of gravel and pebbles. Scrape down the bowl one last time, and make sure no clumps of flour are hiding in the bottom.

Dump the clumps of dough onto your work surface, and squeeze them together until they form a cohesive dough. Flatten the dough into a 9-inch circle, wrap in plastic or parchment, and chill for 30 minutes before continuing.

4   Place a large sheet of parchment paper on your work surface, about the size of a baking sheet. Have a second parchment sheet the same size ready. Remove the dough from the refrigerator and place it in the center of the first parchment sheet. Top with the second parchment sheet, and flatten the dough slightly. Using a rolling pin, and starting from the edge closest to you, roll gently but firmly to the edge opposite you and then back again twice. Be careful not to roll the pin off the edge of the dough, or the dough will stick to the paper. Turn the dough, between the parchment paper, a quarter turn and roll up and back again twice. Repeat rolling up and back and turning until the dough is ¼ inch thick.

5   If the paper creases into the dough, gently peel back the paper, straighten it out, and smooth it back on top of the dough. You'll need to do this several times during the rolling process. If the dough gets too soft and squishy while you are rolling, transfer it to a baking sheet (still between the parchment paper) and refrigerate for 10 to 15 minutes, until cool but flexible.

6   Peel off the top sheet of parchment. If the dough is soft and sticky, refrigerate for 15 minutes. Using the cookie cutters, press down firmly to cut out the shapes (see photo). Cut them as close together as possible. Using a small offset spatula, lift the shapes off the parchment paper and transfer to the prepared pans, spacing them about 1 inch apart. Press all the dough scraps together, roll the dough out, and cut out more shapes.

7   Place 1 baking sheet on each oven rack. Bake for 8 minutes, then, using oven mitts, switch the pans between the oven racks. Bake for another 5 to 9 minutes, until the cookies are golden brown around the edges and lightly golden in the center. Using oven mitts, transfer the pans to the cooling racks and let the cookies cool completely before decorating. You may need to reuse the pans to finish baking all the cookies. Let the pans cool before you put more dough on them for baking.

8   Make the icing. Sift the powdered sugar into another medium bowl. Put the meringue powder and water in a large bowl. Make sure the bowl and your mixer beaters are very clean so the icing will whip up nicely. Beat the meringue on medium speed for about 1 minute, then turn the mixer to high and continue to whip until the mixture looks like whipped cream and has formed soft peaks.

9 With the mixer on medium speed, add the sifted sugar, about ¼ cup at a time, shaking it gently over the bowl and letting it blend in slowly. Once all the sugar has been added, turn the mixer to high speed and continue to beat for 1 to 2 minutes, until the mixture is very fluffy and shiny and forms firm peaks. Turn off the mixer and check the peaks again. At this point, the slope should be nearly vertical.

10 Divide the icing among small bowls—the number depends on how many different colors of icing you want. Color each bowl of icing a different color by stirring in a few drops of food coloring. You can even make your own "custom" colors by combining food colorings. Cover each bowl with a damp, wrung-out paper towel and top with a piece of plastic wrap until you are ready to decorate, or a hard skin will form on top.

11 Using a small offset spatula, spread the icing over the cookies, wiping the spatula clean each time you switch to a different colored icing. You can also pipe icing: Spoon some icing into a small disposable piping bag, cut a tiny hole in the bottom, and squeeze the bag gently to create patterns and shapes on your cookies. Or fill another icing tool, such as a squeeze bottle, and frost the cookies. While the icing is wet, add the sprinkles or other decorations as desired. Let the icing dry for 1 to 2 hours. It will harden. Once it is hard, you can stack the cookies in an airtight container and store them at room temperature for up to 3 weeks.

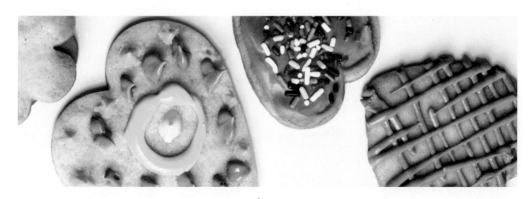

Ingredients

½ cup (1 stick) unsalted butter, softened

½ cup firmly packed light brown sugar

¼ cup plus 1 tablespoon granulated sugar

1 large egg

1 teaspoon pure vanilla extract

1 cup unbleached all-purpose flour

¼ teaspoon baking soda

¼ teaspoon baking powder

¼ teaspoon salt

¾ cup old-fashioned rolled oats

¾ cup dried sour cherries

Cherry
Oatmeal Cookies

MAKES ABOUT 50 COOKIES

This variation on the classic oatmeal cookie is crisp at the edges, soft in the center, and plump with dried sour cherries. The tart cherries are the ideal contrast to the sweetly comforting dough, but you can substitute raisins, dried cranberries, or any other moist dried fruit you like.

1   Preheat the oven to 350°F and position an oven rack in the center of the oven. Line 2 baking sheets with parchment paper.

2   Place the butter, brown sugar, and granulated sugar in the bowl of a stand mixer and beat on medium speed until smooth and blended, about 2 minutes. You can also use a hand mixer and a medium bowl, although you may need to beat the mixture a little longer to achieve the same results. Scrape down the bowl with a spatula. Add the egg and vanilla and blend well.

3   In a medium bowl, whisk together the flour, baking soda, baking powder, and salt. Add to the butter mixture all at once. Turn the mixer to the lowest speed and blend slowly, just until there are no more patches of flour. Scrape down the bowl.

4   Add the oats and cherries and blend on low just until combined. Remove the bowl from the mixer and stir gently a few times with the spatula to make sure there are no more

patches of unincorporated flour or butter lurking near the bottom of the bowl.

5   Using a small ice-cream scoop or a spoon, portion tablespoon-size mounds onto the prepared baking sheets, spacing them about 2 inches apart. Bake the cookies 1 sheet at a time, rotating the sheet halfway through, for 13 to 16 minutes, until the cookies are golden brown at the edges and still a bit pale in the center. Transfer to a cooling rack and let the cookies cool completely.

Variation: Cherry–Chocolate Chip Oatmeal Cookies Add ½ to ¾ cup chocolate chips (or your favorite eating chocolate cut into ¼-inch chunks) to the dough with the oats and dried cherries. Milk chocolate or white chocolate chips may be substituted for dark chocolate if you like, or use a combination of all three. Bake as directed.

Ingredients

1 cup (2 sticks) unsalted butter, softened

4 large eggs, at room temperature

1 tablespoon pure vanilla extract

1 cup canola or corn oil

4 cups unbleached all-purpose flour

2 cups sugar

2 cups tightly packed light brown sugar

2¼ cups old-fashioned rolled oats or quick oats (not instant)

2 teaspoons salt

2 teaspoons baking soda

2½ cups Kellogg's Corn Flakes (for best results, stick to this brand)

1 (12-ounce) bag miniature semisweet chocolate chips

Secret Ingredient
Chocolate Chip Cookies

MAKES ABOUT 25 BIG COOKIES

These are chewy yet crispy, sweet yet salty, oatmeal-like yet packed with chocolate chips. You can vary the size of the finished cookies by using a larger or smaller ice-cream scoop.

1   Position 1 oven rack in the top third of the oven and 1 oven rack in the bottom third of the oven, and preheat the oven to 350°F. Line 2 baking sheets with parchment paper.

2   Put the butter, eggs, and vanilla in a large bowl and stir with a wooden spoon until blended. Add the oil and beat well until combined. It will look like a mess, but that's okay.

3   Put the flour, sugar, brown sugar, oats, salt, and baking soda in another large bowl and whisk until blended. Add the dry ingredients to the butter mixture and stir well with the spoon. You can even use your hands to squish all the ingredients together. Sometimes your hands are the best tools.

4   Put the corn flakes into the resealable plastic bag, squeeze out the air, and seal the top. Squeeze the bag until the flakes are broken into tiny pieces (do not use a food processor; it grinds the flakes too small). Add the crushed flakes and chocolate chips to the dough and stir until evenly blended.

5   Use a large (3 tablespoons) or small (1 tablespoon) ice-cream scoop to shape the dough into cookies. You can also shape the dough by measuring out level tablespoons—3 for each big cookie, 1 for each smaller cookie—and then rolling the dough between your palms into balls.

6   If you are making large cookies, bake only 6 at a time on each baking sheet, spacing the balls about 4 inches apart. These cookies spread when they bake, and if you put too many on the pan, they will run together. If you are making the smaller cookies, you can fit 12 cookies on each pan. Space them about 2 inches apart into 4 rows with 3 cookies in each row. Press down on each ball with your palm to flatten slightly.

7   Place 1 baking sheet on each oven rack. Bake the large cookies for 7 minutes or the smaller cookies for 6 minutes. Using oven mitts, switch the pans between the oven racks. Bake until light golden brown, another 7 to 8 minutes for the large cookies, or 6 to 7 minutes for the smaller cookies.

8   Using oven mitts, transfer the pans to the cooling racks and let the cookies cool completely (if you can wait that long). You may need to reuse the pans to finish baking all the cookies. Let the pans cool before you put more dough on them for baking. Store the cookies in an airtight container or resealable plastic bag for up to 1 week.

9   You can bake some of the cookies today, and freeze the rest of the dough balls for another day. Put the balls close together on a pan and freeze for 30 minutes, or until hard. Transfer the frozen balls to a resealable plastic freezer bag, and freeze for up to 3 months. To bake, take out as many cookies as you need, and space them on parchment-lined baking sheets as directed. Let them thaw for 15 minutes, then press down on them to flatten slightly, and bake as directed.

Ingredients

1 cup (2 sticks) unsalted butter, softened

½ cup powdered sugar

1½ tablespoons pure vanilla extract

2¼ cups unbleached all-purpose flour to finish

1½ cups powdered sugar

Smile
Cookies

MAKES ABOUT 45 COOKIES

Your friends will be smiling when you share these cookies with them. They are a little messy to eat, but well worth it.

1   Position 1 oven rack in the top third of the oven and 1 oven rack in the bottom third of the oven, and preheat the oven to 350°F. Line 2 baking sheets with parchment paper.

2   Put the butter and sugar in a bowl. Using the mixer, beat for about 1 minute on low speed. Turn up the speed to medium and beat for 5 to 6 minutes, until very light, almost white, in color. Turn off the mixer. Using a spatula, scrape down the sides of the bowl. Add the vanilla and mix on medium for another 30 seconds. Turn off the mixer. Scrape down the bowl.

3   Add the flour and mix on low speed just until the flour is completely blended. Scrape down the bowl one last time, and make sure no clumps of flour are hiding in the bottom.

4   To shape each cookie, break off a piece of dough that measures 1 level tablespoon. Roll the pieces on your work surface back and forth with your fingertips, shaping them into logs that are 3 inches long. As you do this, put a little extra pressure at the ends of the logs, so they are pointed. Place on a prepared baking sheet, shaping each log into a smile. Repeat to make

more smiles, spacing them 1 inch apart on the baking sheets.

5   Place 1 baking sheet on each oven rack. Bake for 7 minutes, then, using oven mitts, switch the pans between the oven racks. Bake for another 8 to 9 minutes, until the cookies are a light sand color and firm to the touch. They should be golden brown across the bottom and around the edges, but still fairly light on top. Using oven mitts, transfer the pans to the cooling racks and let the cookies cool on the pans for 10 minutes.

6   Wash and dry the large bowl. Sift the powdered sugar into the bowl. While the cookies are still warm, roll each one in the sugar until it is completely coated, then return it to the pan to finish cooling. When the cookies are cool, roll them in the powdered sugar again so they are thickly coated and silky white. Store in an airtight container at room temperature for up to 1 week. If the powdered sugar becomes moist or soaks into the cookies, roll them again in powdered sugar just before serving.

Ingredients

3 large egg whites

¾ cup sugar

**Colored sugar or candy-coated
almonds, for decorating**

Meringue
Crispies

MAKES ABOUT 60 FUN-SHAPED COOKIES

When you bite into these cookies they are very crunchy, and then they melt in your mouth like cotton candy. They are also delicious dipped into melted chocolate. Make these on a dry day, or they will end up chewy instead of crispy. The variation makes fun treats for a Halloween party.

1   Position 1 oven rack in the top third of the oven and 1 oven rack in the bottom third of the oven, and preheat the oven to 225°F. Line 2 baking sheets with parchment paper.

2   Be sure your bowl and beaters are very clean and there is not a speck of yolk in the egg whites. Any dirt or grease will prevent the whites from whipping. Put the egg whites in a large bowl. Using the mixer, beat on medium speed until they look like whipped cream and form soft peaks. To check, turn off the mixer, lift the beaters straight out, and then turn them upside down. The slope leading to the tip should be soft and barely holding its shape.

3   With the mixer on medium speed, add the sugar, about ¼ cup at a time, shaking it gently over the bowl and letting it blend in slowly. Once all the sugar has been added, turn the mixer to high speed and continue to beat for 1 to 2 minutes, until the mixture is very fluffy and shiny and forms firm peaks. This is a meringue. Turn off the mixer and check the peaks again. At this point, the slope should be nearly vertical.

4   Put the tip into a pastry bag. Spoon the meringue into the bag until it is half full. Grasp the bag just above the mound of meringue and twist it 3 times (this prevents the mixture from coming out the wrong end of the bag).

5   Squeeze from the twisted part of the bag, while guiding the bag with a couple of fingers near the tip. Pipe the meringue onto the prepared baking sheets into any shape you like: letters of the alphabet, rounds, or zigzags, for example. Keep the tip of the bag about 1 inch from the surface of the pan, and let the meringue fall out of the bag onto the pan in a thick rope.

6   Once the bag is empty, untwist, open the top, and fill with the remaining meringue. Retwist and continue piping until you have used all the meringue. If you like, sprinkle the cookies with colored sugar.

7   Place 1 baking sheet on each oven rack. Bake for 1 hour. Turn off the oven and leave the pans inside overnight to finish drying the meringues. Tape a note to the oven door reminding your family not to turn on the oven!

8   In the morning, remove the cookies from the oven and store them in an airtight container at room temperature. They will keep for up to 8 weeks, as long as they are kept dry.

Variation: Rattling Meringue Bones and Fingers
For Bones: Pipe the meringue into a stretched version of dog-bone treats.

For Fingers: Pipe a straight line with a knobby center for the knuckle and tapered end for the fingernail. Just before baking, set a colored candy almond or an almond slice into the meringue at the tapered end for a fingernail. Once the "fingers" have dried, dip the end opposite the fingernail into melted red coating chocolate for blood. Pipe a fancy ring on the finger with melted colored coating chocolate, and embellish it with "jewels" of colored sugars, dragées, or candy pearls.

Classic
Lemon Bars

MAKES 36 (1½-INCH) SQUARES

Eyes light up at the sight of these tart and refreshing favorites. A soft, puckery lemon filling atop a vanilla-scented short crust is just the ticket after a rich winter meal, and it is also a refreshing treat on a hot summer day. Okay, okay, it's great anytime. Surprisingly easy to make, these bars deliver a lot of satisfaction for the amount of elbow grease invested. Of course, lemon is the classic, but you could substitute lime juice as well. Or, for a more exotic version, try an equal amount of passion fruit juice instead of the lemon juice.

1   To mix the dough using a food processor: Place the flour, sugar, and salt in the bowl of a food processor. Pulse 5 times to blend. Add the cold butter pieces and pulse 6 to 8 times, just until the butter is the size of large peas. In the small bowl, whisk together the egg yolks, vanilla, and 1 teaspoon water. Add to the butter mixture, then process just until the dough begins to form small clumps, 5 to 10 seconds. Do not let the dough form a ball. Test the dough by squeezing a handful of clumps—when you open your hand, they should hold together. If they are crumbly and fall apart, sprinkle 1 teaspoon water over the dough and pulse several times, then test again. Repeat, if necessary.

························
Ingredients

Crust

1¼ cups unbleached all-purpose flour

¼ cup sugar

¼ teaspoon salt

½ cup (1 stick) cold unsalted butter, cut into ½-inch pieces

2 large egg yolks

2 teaspoons pure vanilla extract

1 to 3 teaspoons water

Filling

4 large eggs

2 cups granulated sugar

5 tablespoons unbleached all-purpose flour

⅔ cup strained freshly squeezed lemon juice

Confectioners' sugar, for dusting (optional)

························

To mix the dough by hand: Place the flour, sugar, and salt in the medium bowl and blend well with a whisk. Add the cold butter pieces and toss until they are lightly coated with the flour. Use the pastry blender or your fingertips to cut the butter into the flour until the mixture resembles bread crumbs or crushed crackers. If at any time during this process the butter softens and becomes warm, place the bowl in the freezer for 10 minutes before continuing. In the small bowl, whisk together the egg yolks, vanilla, and 1 teaspoon water. Add to the dry ingredients and toss between your fingertips or with a fork 20 to 30 times to evenly distribute the moisture. The dough will still look very crumbly, but if the mixture is squeezed in your hand, it should hold together. If not, sprinkle another teaspoon of water over the top and toss to blend. Repeat, if necessary.

2   Preheat the oven to 350°F and position an oven rack in the center. Line a 9-inch square baking pan with foil across the bottom and up all 4 sides, then lightly coat with melted butter, oil, or high-heat canola-oil spray.

3   With a spatula, scrape the dough into the prepared pan and press it into an even layer across the bottom of the pan. Chill for 30 minutes.

4   Bake the chilled crust for 35 to 45 minutes, until golden brown. Transfer to a rack and allow to cool for 20 minutes. Reduce the oven temperature to 300°F.

5   Make the filling. Whisk the eggs and granulated sugar together in a medium bowl. Whisk in the flour until there are no lumps. Whisk in the lemon juice. Pour the filling over the crust. Bake for 50 to 60 minutes, until the filling is set and does not jiggle when you tap the side of the pan. Transfer to a rack to cool completely. When cool, refrigerate for 1 hour.

6   To serve, grasp the foil and lift the cookies out of the pan. Set them on a cutting surface. Gently peel back the foil, using the tip of a thin knife or a small spatula to help separate the bars from the foil if necessary. Cut into 1½-inch squares and transfer to a serving plate or storage container. Just before serving, use a fine-mesh strainer to dust confectioners' sugar over the tops, if using. (Wait until the last minute to do this or the confectioners' sugar will soak into the filling and look blotchy.)

Peanut Butter Thumbprints

with Peanut Caramel

MAKES ABOUT 50 COOKIES

These are your favorite peanut butter cookies, all dressed up and ready for a party. Their centers are filled with a mixture of salted peanuts coated with caramel sauce, and their tops can be drizzled with chocolate. You'll end up with more peanut caramel sauce than you need for this recipe, but it's hard to make it in a smaller quantity. Store any extra in the refrigerator (it keeps for several weeks) and use it whenever the mood strikes—for ice cream, fondue, toast . . . It won't hang around for long. Neither will the cookies.

1   Preheat the oven to 350°F and position 2 oven racks in the upper and lower thirds of the oven. Line 2 baking sheets with parchment paper.

2   Mix the dough. Place the butter, brown sugar, and granulated sugar in the bowl of the stand mixer and beat on medium speed until smooth and blended, about 2 minutes. You can also use a hand mixer and a medium bowl, although you may need to beat the mixture a little longer to achieve the same results. Scrape down the bowl with a spatula. Add the egg and vanilla and blend well. Scrape down the bowl again. Add the peanut butter, beat until well blended, and scrape down the bowl once more.

Dough

½ cup (1 stick) unsalted butter, softened

½ cup firmly packed light brown sugar

½ cup granulated sugar

1 large egg

1 teaspoon pure vanilla extract

¾ cup creamy salted peanut butter, at room temperature

1¾ cups unbleached all-purpose flour

½ teaspoon baking soda

¼ teaspoon salt

Peanut Caramel

1 cup heavy whipping cream

½ cup water

1 cup granulated sugar

1 tablespoon light corn syrup

⅛ teaspoon salt

¾ cup finely chopped roasted salted peanuts

4 ounces semisweet or bittersweet chocolate, finely chopped and melted (optional)

3   In a medium bowl, whisk together the flour, baking soda, and salt. Add to the butter mixture all at once. Turn the mixer to the lowest speed and blend slowly, just until there are no more patches of flour. Scrape down the bowl. Remove the bowl from the mixer and stir gently a few times with the spatula to make sure there are no patches of unincorporated flour or butter lurking near the bottom of the bowl.

4   Use the ice-cream scoop to portion tablespoon-size mounds onto the prepared baking sheets, spacing them about 1½ inches apart. Or use a spoon to portion the dough, then roll each piece into a ball between your hands and place on the prepared sheets, about 20 cookies per sheet. Use the rounded handle end of a wooden spoon (or another kitchen utensil) to make a depression, about an inch in diameter, in the center of each cookie.

5   Bake the cookies, switching the sheets between the racks and rotating each front to back halfway through, for 13 to 16 minutes, until they are lightly golden brown all over and a bit darker at the edges. Transfer to a cooling rack. Immediately reinforce the depression in each cookie using the same kitchen utensil. Be careful not to push so hard that you crack the cookie or break through to the baking sheet. Cool and reline one of the baking sheets, and bake the remaining cookie dough as directed. Let the cookies cool completely.

6   Make the peanut caramel. Microwave the cream in a small, microwave-safe bowl just until hot. Set aside. Place the water in a medium saucepan and add the sugar, corn syrup, and salt. (The pan will seem too large, but when the cream is added the mixture will rise dramatically.) Cook the sugar mixture over medium heat, stirring occasionally with a heatproof spatula, until the sugar dissolves. Set the hot cream on the counter next to the stovetop. Turn the heat to high and cook the sugar mixture, occasionally swirling the pan (not stirring) so that the sugar cooks evenly, until it turns a golden brown. Immediately turn off the heat and whisk in the cream, adding it in a slow, steady stream. Whisk to blend the caramel well. Pour into the heatproof bowl and let cool until warm and pourable (if it becomes cold and thick, simply reheat in the microwave until it is fluid again). Stir in the peanuts.

7   Fill the cookies. Spoon the peanut caramel into the depressions of each cookie. Allow the filling to cool and set for an hour before finishing with the chocolate (if using). Cover and refrigerate any leftover peanut caramel to use another day.

8   Top with the chocolate. Place the melted chocolate in a small resealable plastic bag. Snip a small hole in the corner of the bag and stripe the chocolate over the top of the cookies. Allow the chocolate to cool and harden completely before transferring the cookies to a storage container.

¼ cup granulated sugar

1 tablespoon good-quality Earl Grey tea leaves

½ cup (1 stick) cold unsalted butter, cut into ½-inch pieces

¾ cup unbleached all-purpose flour

3 tablespoons unsweetened cocoa powder, either Dutch-process or natural

⅛ teaspoon salt

3 tablespoons sanding or decorator's sugar (optional)

....

Chocolate–Earl Grey
Shortbread Coins

MAKES ABOUT 36 COOKIES

Deeply chocolaty and delicately nubby from the texture of Earl Grey tea leaves, these are cookies for adults. Earl Grey, black tea flavored with bergamot oil (from a variety of bitter orange called bergamot), is an inspired match for dark chocolate. For the best flavor, use a top-quality bulk tea, which can often be purchased at your local coffee house. Serve the cookies with a cup of the tea—or any time you want a sophisticated cookie. Without tea leaves, they are a wonderful chocolate shortbread cookie that even children will love. The dough can also be rolled out and cut into shapes.

1   Place the granulated sugar and tea leaves in the bowl of the food processor and grind for 1 minute, or until the leaves are very finely chopped. Add the butter, flour, cocoa, and salt and process for about 45 seconds. Scrape down the bowl and break up any large clumps with the spatula. Process for another 15 to 30 seconds, until the dough looks uniformly dark and forms large, shaggy clumps. Dump the dough out onto a work surface and knead gently several times, just to bring it together.

2   Squeeze the dough into a log about 12 inches long and about 1 inch in diameter, and gently roll it back and forth until smooth. Don't add flour if the dough is sticky—simply refrigerate the dough for 15 to 20 minutes to firm up the butter, then try again.

3   If you like, sprinkle the sanding sugar on the work surface alongside the log and gently roll the log in the sugar, turning to coat evenly. Cut a piece of plastic wrap several inches longer than the log and center the log at one long edge of the wrap. Roll the log into the wrap so it is tightly bound by the plastic. Twist the ends of the wrap to secure the log and help to create a rounded shape. You can use a cardboard paper towel roll to keep the roll of dough nicely rounded during storage. Just slit the cardboard lengthwise and slip the log inside it to help keep the rounded shape. Refrigerate for 2 hours.

4   Preheat the oven to 300°F and position an oven rack in the center. Line a baking sheet with parchment paper.

5   Remove the cardboard paper towel roll and plastic wrap from the dough log and use a thin knife to slice it into ⅜-inch-thick rounds. Place about 18 cookies 1 inch apart on the prepared baking sheet. Bake, rotating the sheet halfway through the baking time, for 30 minutes, or until the cookies are cooked through and look dry on top. (It's difficult to tell when dark chocolate cookies are done. This is when an oven thermometer and a timer are your best friends in the kitchen.) Transfer the cookies to a cooling rack and let them cool completely.

Almond-Chocolate Spritz Cookies

with Orange Blossom Water

MAKES ABOUT 45 (2-INCH) COOKIES

Buttery spritz cookies, the much-anticipated standard on the holiday cookie platter, deserve to be enjoyed all year-round. Instead of saving these for special occasions, why not make some to enjoy with a cup of tea, as an after-school snack, or with a bowl of ice cream? These are deeply almond due to the inclusion of almond paste, with a lovely tender crumb and enough structure to support a pool of dark chocolate in the center. The orange blossom water, with its delicate perfume of white citrus flowers, lends another subtle layer of flavor. If you can't find orange blossom water, substitute vanilla extract, which will impart its own unique floral notes to the dough.

1   Make the dough. Place the almond paste and sugar in the bowl of a stand mixer (or in a food processor). Beat on medium speed for 1½ to 2 minutes (or process for 45 seconds), until the almond paste is broken into tiny pieces. Add the butter and continue to beat for another 2 minutes (or process for 1 minute), until the mixture is well blended and slightly lighter in color. Scrape down the sides of the bowl with a spatula.

2   Add the egg and yolk and blend well (or process for 15 seconds). Add the orange blossom water and beat another 15 seconds to blend (or process for 5 seconds). Scrape down

. . . .
Ingredients

Dough

½ cup firmly packed almond paste
(do not substitute marzipan)

¾ cup sugar

1¾ sticks unsalted butter, softened

1 large egg plus 1 yolk

1 teaspoon orange blossom water
or pure vanilla extract

2 cups unbleached all-purpose
flour

Pinch of salt

Chocolate Filling

2 ounces semisweet or bittersweet
chocolate (up to 56 percent
cacao), finely chopped

1 tablespoon heavy whipping
cream

. . . .

the sides of the bowl. Add the flour and salt. Turn the mixer to the lowest speed and blend slowly (or process for 10 to 15 seconds), just until there are no more patches of flour. Remove the bowl and stir gently a few times with the spatula to make sure there are no patches of unincorporated flour or butter lurking near the bottom of the bowl.

3   Shape the dough. Line 2 baking sheets with parchment paper. Immediately spoon half of the dough into the pastry bag fitted with the star tip. Pipe rosettes on the prepared baking sheets, spacing the cookies about 1 inch apart. (Alternatively, use a cookie press according to the manufacturer's instructions.) The rosettes should be about ½ inch thick and about 1¾ inches in diameter. Repeat with the remaining dough. Chill the baking sheets in the refrigerator for 30 minutes.

4   Preheat the oven to 350°F and position 2 oven racks in the upper and lower thirds of the oven.

5   Bake the cookies, switching the sheets between the racks and rotating each front to back halfway through, for 15 to 20 minutes, until the cookies are rich, golden brown around the edges and across the bottom. Transfer to a cooling rack.

6   Immediately use the rounded handle end of a wooden spoon (or another kitchen utensil) to make a depression in the center of each cookie about ½ inch across. Be careful not to push so hard that you crack the cookie or break through to the baking sheet. Let the cookies cool completely.

7   Fill the cookies. Place the chopped chocolate and cream in a microwave-safe bowl and microwave on low for 30 seconds. Stir the mixture. Heat again for 30 seconds and stir until smooth. If there are still lumps, heat again for 30 seconds. Once smooth, spoon a little chocolate into each depression in the cookies. Allow the filling to cool and set completely.

Chocolate Mint Brownies

with White Chocolate Chunks

MAKES 16 (2-INCH) BROWNIES

Rich, dark, fudgy, and slightly chewy, these homemade brownies are always a hit, so much better than anything you can buy. Serve cold with a glass of milk, or warm from the oven with a scoop of ice cream. Like a simple black dress, they can be accessorized to match any occasion. For a casual snack, serve them right out of the pan. For something a bit dressier, dust the brownies with a layer of confectioners' sugar, then use a stencil and cocoa powder for a contrasting design. Inspired by Jackson Pollock? Drizzle melted white chocolate wildly over the top.

1   Preheat the oven to 350°F and position an oven rack in the center. Line an 8-inch square baking pan with foil or parchment paper across the bottom and up two of the sides, then lightly coat with unflavored oil or high-heat canola-oil spray.

2   Bring 2 inches of water to a boil in the bottom of a double boiler. Place the butter, semisweet chocolate, and unsweetened chocolate in the top of the double boiler (off the heat). Turn off the heat, then set the butter and chocolate over the steaming water. Stir occasionally with a spatula until the chocolate is melted and the mixture is smooth.

3   Remove the chocolate mixture from the heat and whisk in the sugar. Whisk in the eggs, one at a time, stirring well to incorporate each before adding the next. Stir in the mint extract.

Ingredients

½ cup (1 stick) unsalted butter, cut into ½-inch pieces

4 ounces semisweet or bittersweet chocolate (up to 64 percent cacao), finely chopped

2 ounces unsweetened chocolate, finely chopped

1 cup sugar

2 large eggs, at room temperature

¾ teaspoon pure mint extract

½ cup unbleached all-purpose flour

Pinch of salt

5½ ounces white chocolate, chopped into ¼-inch pieces

Whisk in the flour and salt. Continue to stir until the mixture changes from dull and broken-looking to smooth and shiny, about 1 minute. Whisk in 4 ounces of the white chocolate.

4   Scrape the batter into the prepared pan and spread evenly. Bake for 35 to 40 minutes, until a skewer inserted into the center of the brownies comes out with a few moist crumbs clinging to it (do not overbake). Transfer to a rack and cool completely.

5   Melt the remaining 1½ ounces of the white chocolate over a double boiler. Pipe or stripe it over the top of the cooled brownies in any pattern you like. Let the white chocolate cool and harden before cutting the brownies.

6   Run a thin knife or flexible spatula around the edges of the pan to loosen the brownies. To remove the brownies from the pan, grasp the foil or parchment paper extending up the sides and pull gently upward. Set the brownies on a cutting surface and use a chef's knife to cut into 16 equal pieces. Since these are fudgy, it's a good idea to keep a hot, wrung-out towel nearby so you can wipe the knife clean between slices. You could also serve the brownies right out of the pan, if you like, pressing a piece of plastic wrap against any cut surfaces and across the top to keep them fresh.

Cappuccino Biscotti

with Hazelnuts and Chocolate

MAKES ABOUT 45 BISCOTTI

Biscotti—twice-baked, super-crunchy Italian favorites—are made for dunking into a steaming cup of coffee, tea, or hot chocolate. They can often be too hard to enjoy out of hand, though. This particular style of biscotti, with a bit of butter added for additional flavor and a softer texture, is great for snacking, whether dipped or dunked. They are good make-ahead cookies and keep well in an airtight container for weeks. Theoretically. You probably won't be able to keep them around long enough to find out. Many variations can be made from this recipe by leaving out the espresso powder, changing the nuts to almonds, walnuts, or pistachios, adding ½ cup of dried fruit (such as raisins or cranberries), and/or leaving out or changing the type of chocolate chips.

1 Preheat the oven to 350°F and position an oven rack in the center.

2 In a small bowl, stir together the espresso powder and warm water until the powder is dissolved. Set aside.

3 Place the butter and granulated sugar in the bowl of a stand mixer and beat on medium speed until smooth and slightly lightened in color, 2 to 3 minutes. You can also use a hand mixer and a medium bowl, although you may need to beat the mixture a little longer to achieve the same results. Add the espresso mixture and blend well. Scrape down the bowl with

....

Ingredients

1½ tablespoons instant espresso powder

2 teaspoons warm water

½ cup (1 stick) unsalted butter, softened

⅔ cup granulated sugar

3 large eggs, at room temperature

2¾ cups unbleached all-purpose flour

½ teaspoon baking powder

¼ teaspoon salt

1 cup chopped skinned toasted hazelnuts

5 ounces good-quality semisweet or bittersweet chocolate, cut into ¼-inch chunks, or 1 cup mini chocolate chips

½ cup superfine sugar (optional)

½ teaspoon ground cinnamon (optional)

....

a spatula. Add the eggs, one at a time, beating well (15 to 20 seconds) and scraping down the sides of the bowl after each addition.

4   In a medium bowl, whisk together the flour, baking powder, and salt. Add to the butter mixture all at once. Turn the mixer to the lowest speed and blend slowly, just until there are no more patches of flour. Turn off the mixer and scrape down the bowl.

5   Add the hazelnuts and chocolate chips and mix on low just until blended. Remove the bowl from the mixer and stir gently a few times with a spatula to make sure the nuts and chips are evenly distributed and there are no patches of unincorporated flour or butter lurking near the bottom of the bowl.

6   Shape and bake the dough: Divide the dough in half. On a work surface lightly dusted with flour, gently squeeze and roll each piece to shape into logs about 13 inches long. Line 1 baking sheet with parchment paper. Place the logs on the sheet about 4 inches apart. Press down on the logs, flattening them slightly until they are each about 2 inches across the top. Place a second baking sheet under the first (to prevent the bottoms of the logs from browning too quickly). Bake for 30 to 35 minutes, until the logs are firm to the touch and lightly golden brown. Transfer the pan to a cooling rack and let the logs cool completely. (If you attempt to slice them while warm, the chocolate will smear and the cookies will look messy.)

7   Cut the logs and bake them a second time: Turn the oven down to 275°F and position two racks in the top and bottom thirds of the oven. Carefully transfer the cookie logs to a cutting surface. Use the serrated knife to slice the logs on a slight diagonal into cookies ⅜ inch thick. Line the second baking sheet with parchment paper. Place the cookies, cut side down, on the parchment-lined sheets (you'll need both sheets to hold all the cookies). Toast the cookies in the oven, switching the sheets between the racks and rotating each front to back halfway through, for 30 to 40 minutes, until dry and lightly tinged with color. Transfer to a cooling rack.

8   While the cookies are toasting, prepare the finishing sugar if you like. Whisk together the superfine sugar and cinnamon in a clean medium bowl. As soon as the cookies are out of the oven and on the rack, immediately roll them in the cinnamon sugar and return to the baking sheet to cool completely.

Ingredients

Crust

1½ cups fine graham cracker crumbs

1 tablespoon sugar

6 tablespoons (¾ stick) unsalted butter, melted

Brownie Filling

6 ounces semisweet chocolate

½ cup (1 stick) unsalted butter, cut into pieces

¾ cup sugar

2 large eggs, at room temperature

2 teaspoons pure vanilla extract

½ cup unbleached all-purpose flour

⅛ teaspoon salt

½ cup milk chocolate chips

1¼ cups mini marshmallows

Brownie

S'mores Bars

MAKES 36 TREATS

Don't completely cover the surface of the brownies with marshmallows, or they will be impossible to cut through after baking. If you want extra marshmallows, add them to the top after you cut the bars.

1   Position an oven rack in the center of the oven, and preheat the oven to 350°F. Turn a 9-inch square baking pan upside down and mold a piece of aluminum foil to the outside. You should have about an inch of overhang around the edges. Slide the foil off the pan bottom, and turn the pan right side up. Slip the foil inside the pan. Fold down any foil that extends past the top edges over the outside. Lightly butter the foil, or use pan spray.

2   Place the graham cracker crumbs and sugar in a medium bowl. Pour the melted butter over the cookie crumbs and stir with a silicone spatula until the mixture is evenly moistened. Smash any lumps that form.

3   Scrape the mixture into the prepared pan and use your clean fingers to press it into an even layer over the bottom of the pan.

4   Bake for 10 minutes. Using oven mitts, transfer the pan to a cooling rack and let cool for 15 minutes. Leave the oven on.

5   Put the chocolate on the cutting board. Using a serrated knife, chop the chocolate into small pieces. Put the butter in a medium saucepan, place over low heat, and heat until it melts. Turn off the heat, and move the pan to a heatproof surface. Add the chocolate to the pan, let it sit for 2 minutes, then whisk until blended. The chocolate should be very smooth. If it is still lumpy, let it sit for another minute or two, then whisk again. Scrape the chocolate mixture into a large bowl.

6   Whisk the sugar into the chocolate mixture until fully blended. Whisk in the eggs, one at a time, blending well after each egg is added. Whisk in the vanilla. Finally, whisk in the flour and salt. Whisk slowly at first, then faster, until the batter is smooth and shiny. It will be thick. Stir in the chocolate chips.

7   Using a spatula, scrape the batter into the crust and smooth the top. Bake for 25 minutes. Using oven mitts, remove the pan from the oven, set it on a heat proof surface, and close the oven door. Carefully sprinkle the mini marshmallows evenly over the top. With your hand covered by an oven mitt, gently press on the marshmallows just once so they stick to the brownie filling.

8   Return the pan to the oven and continue to bake for another 15 minutes, or until the brownie mixture feels firm when lightly pressed, a toothpick inserted into the center comes out with a few moist crumbs on it, and the marshmallows are golden brown. Using oven mitts, transfer to a cooling rack and let cool completely.

9   To remove the big brownie from the pan, grasp the foil at the top in 2 places opposite each other and gently pull upward. Set the big brownie on a cutting board, and then gently peel back the foil.

10 Spray the chef's knife with a little pan spray so the sticky brownies won't cling to it when you cut them. Keep a warm, damp towel handy so you can wipe and respray the knife when it gets too messy. Starting at one side, cut the square into 6 equal strips. Then, cut 6 equal strips in the opposite direction. You will have 36 brownies. Of course, you can cut the brownies larger or smaller, if you like. Lift the brownies off the foil bottom. Store in an airtight container or a resealable plastic bag for up to 5 days.

Ingredients

½ cup (1 stick) unsalted butter, softened

1 cup tightly packed light brown sugar

1 large egg, at room temperature

2 teaspoons pure vanilla extract

1¼ cups unbleached all-purpose flour

1 teaspoon baking powder

¼ teaspoon salt

½ cup milk chocolate chips

½ cup toffee baking bits

Milk Chocolate
Toffee Bars

MAKES 36 CHEWY SQUARES

These squares are soft and chewy and filled with lots of caramely flavors. The crunchy little toffee bits melt into pools of sweetness in the dough.

1   Position an oven rack in the center of the oven, and preheat the oven to 350°F. Turn an 8-inch square baking pan upside down and mold a piece of aluminum foil to the outside. You should have about an inch of overhang around the edges. Slide the foil off the pan bottom, and turn the pan right side up. Slip the foil inside the pan. Fold down any foil that extends past the top edges over the outside. Lightly butter the foil, or use pan spray.

2   Put the butter and sugar in a large bowl. Using a mixer, beat on low speed for 1 minute. Turn up the speed to medium and beat for another minute. The mixture should be blended and smooth. Turn off the mixer. Using a spatula, scrape down the sides of the bowl. Add the egg and vanilla and beat on medium-low speed until well blended. Turn off the mixer. Scrape down the sides of the bowl.

3   Put the flour, baking powder, and salt in a medium bowl and whisk until blended. Add the dry ingredients to the butter mixture and beat on low speed just until no patches of flour are visible. Add the chocolate chips and toffee bits and

continue to beat on low until they are evenly blended in the mixture.

4   Using a spatula, scrape the dough into the prepared pan, and smooth the top in an even layer. Bake for 35 to 40 minutes, until the top is golden brown. Using oven mitts, transfer the pan to a cooling rack and let cool completely.

5   To remove the big bar from the pan, grasp the foil at the top in 2 places opposite each other and gently pull upward. Set the big bar on a cutting board, and gently peel off the foil. Using a chef's knife, and starting at one side, cut the square into 6 equal strips. Then cut 6 equal strips in the opposite direction. You will have 36 bars. Of course, you can cut the cookies larger or smaller, if you like. Store in an airtight container or a resealable plastic bag for up to 4 days.

Ingredients

3 tablespoons unsalted butter, cut into ½-inch pieces

1 tablespoon coffee liqueur or cooled brewed coffee

6 ounces 70 percent cacao bittersweet chocolate, finely chopped

2 large eggs

½ cup plus ½ cup granulated sugar

¾ cup unbleached all-purpose flour

½ cup whole almonds, toasted and cooled completely

¾ teaspoon ground cinnamon

½ teaspoon baking powder

¼ teaspoon ancho chile powder (optional)

¾ cup unsifted confectioners' sugar

Mexican Chocolate
Crackle Cookies

MAKES ABOUT 45 COOKIES

This is a great place to use that extra-dark 70 percent cacao chocolate you've had your eye on. Because of how they are mixed, the cookies are very chocolaty, yet surprisingly light and delicate. The touch of chile powder adds an intriguing backnote—not heat exactly, but a sultry earthiness that enhances the chocolate flavor. You can find ancho chile powder in the Mexican spice section at the supermarket or specialty Mexican and Latin American markets. The dough is made using the sponge method—that is, the eggs and sugar are whipped together until very light in texture, then the remaining ingredients are added. Before baking, each ball of dough is coated first in granulated sugar and then in a thick layer of confectioners' sugar. The granulated sugar creates a thin, crisp, outer shell during baking, while the confectioners' sugar adds a cooling sweetness to each bite. As the cookies rise, big chocolate cracks form in the white coating, creating the dramatic, two-tone look of the cookie.

1   Bring 2 inches of water to a boil in the bottom of a double boiler. Place the butter, liqueur, and chocolate in the top of the double boiler (off the heat). Turn off the heat, then set the chocolate over the steaming water. Stir occasionally with a spatula until the chocolate is melted and the mixture is smooth. Remove and let cool slightly while you whip the eggs.

2   Place the eggs and ½ cup of the granulated sugar in the bowl of a mixer and whip on high speed until very light in color and

thick, 5 to 6 minutes. You can also use a hand mixer and a medium bowl, though you may need to beat the mixture a little longer to achieve the same results. Scrape the melted chocolate mixture into the eggs and whip until blended, about 1 minute. Scrape down the sides of the bowl.

3   Place the flour, nuts, cinnamon, baking powder, and chile powder (if using) in a food processor and process until the nuts are very finely chopped, 60 to 90 seconds. Add the flour mixture to the egg mixture and beat on low speed just until combined. Stir gently a few times with a spatula to make sure there are no patches of unincorporated flour or butter lurking near the bottom of the bowl. Cover the dough with plastic and refrigerate for 1 to 2 hours, until firm.

4   Preheat the oven to 325°F and position an oven rack in the center. Line 2 baking sheets with parchment paper.

5   Scoop the chilled dough into tablespoon-size balls using a small ice-cream scoop or a spoon. Place the remaining ½ cup of granulated sugar in a small bowl and the confectioners' sugar in another. Roll each dough ball in the granulated sugar and then in the confectioners' sugar. Be sure to coat the dough generously with the confectioners' sugar—in this instance, more is better. Space the cookies about 1½ inches apart on the prepared baking sheets.

6   Bake the cookies one sheet at a time, rotating the sheet halfway through the baking time, for 11 to 14 minutes, until the cookies are puffed and cracked. If you nudge a cookie, it should slide on the sheet rather than stick. It is better to slightly underbake these cookies than to go too far—when overbaked they are dry and unpalatable. Transfer to a cooling rack and let cool completely.

Ingredients

½ cup plus 2 tablespoons
   sugar

½ cup sifted cake flour

2 large egg whites

¾ teaspoon pure vanilla extract

¼ cup (½ stick) unsalted butter,
   melted

Tuiles

MAKES 13 TO 14 LARGE (4-INCH) ROUND COOKIES, OR 20 TO 25
SMALLER ROUND OR VARIOUSLY SHAPED COOKIES

Thin and shatteringly crisp, a tuile (French for "tile") is a vanilla-scented wafer cookie baked into a thin round, then laid over a rolling pin while warm so that it cools into the gently curved shape of a terra-cotta roof tile. The batter is a snap to make and the cookies bake quickly, but do require your attention while shaping and cooling. Some tips: Bake them on a silicone mat to ensure their easy removal while still warm; watch them carefully so they don't burn; and store them absolutely airtight, as they soften quickly. Bake only a few at a time until you get the hang of shaping the warm cookies.

1   Place the sugar and cake flour in a medium bowl and whisk to blend. Whisk in the egg whites and vanilla until well blended. Whisk in the melted butter until a smooth, thin batter is formed. Cover and refrigerate for 30 minutes.

2   Preheat the oven to 350°F and position an oven rack in the center. Line a baking sheet with a silicone mat. Drop about 1 tablespoon of batter onto the mat. With an offset spatula, spread the batter into a thin circle about 4 inches in diameter. Make 3 more circles, spacing them 3 to 4 inches apart. Alternately, set a stencil on the mat and use the spatula to fill the center, scraping off any excess, so the cookie is the same thickness as the stencil around it. Remove the stencil and repeat with more batter. Bake the tuiles for 7 to 9 minutes, until the edges are golden brown but the center is still pale.

3 Transfer the cookies to a rack and let cool for 1 to 2 minutes, until they can be loosened and lifted from the sheet without tearing. Use a small spatula to loosen the edges and help you lift each warm cookie off the pan and quickly shape them. For tuiles: Drape the warm cookies, smooth side down, over the top of a lightly sprayed or oiled rolling pin or dowel (below). Let cool for 1 minute, then remove and set aside. Repeat until all the cookies are shaped. For bowls: Gently drape the warm cookies over an upside-down custard or coffee cup and use your fingers to press the warm cookie snugly against the mold. For cigarettes:

Turn the warm cookies over so the smooth side is facing upward. Roll them loosely around a pencil, small dowel, or the handle of a wooden spoon or similar kitchen utensil that has been lightly sprayed or oiled (below). Allow the cookies to cool completely before transferring them to an airtight container. Bake additional cookies on a silicone mat on a cool baking sheet (or reuse the same sheets by rinsing under cold water, then wiping dry).

Ingredients

1¾ cups unbleached all-purpose flour

1¾ cups old-fashioned or quick oats (not instant)

1 cup firmly packed light brown sugar

¼ teaspoon salt

1 cup (2 sticks) cold unsalted butter, cut into ½-inch pieces

Filling

1 (16-ounce) jar good-quality seedless raspberry jam

1 cup dried sour cherries

Confectioners' sugar, for dusting

Raspberry-Cherry
Crumble Bars

MAKES 36 (3 BY 1-INCH) BARS

These homey, irresistible bars can be put together in no time, will feed a crowd, and are loved by everyone. The brown sugar–oatmeal crust provides just the right sweetness and crunch against the soft, tart, lightly chewy filling in the center, which is simply a mixture of raspberry jam and dried sour cherries. Pack them in lunches, bring them to bake sales, or serve them warm with ice cream—this is a good recipe to have in your repertoire. Use old-fashioned oats when you want a hearty crunch, or quick oats for a more tender bite, but don't use instant oats or you'll have mush.

1   Preheat the oven to 350°F and position an oven rack in the center. Line a 9 by 13-inch baking pan with foil across the bottom and up the two long sides, then lightly coat with melted butter, oil, or high-heat canola-oil spray.

2   Make the crumble dough. Place the flour, oats, brown sugar, and salt in the bowl of a stand mixer and beat on low speed until evenly mixed (or place in a food processor and process for 5 seconds). Add the cold butter and mix on low speed until the mixture looks like wet sand and starts to form clumps, 5 to 6 minutes (or process for 45 to 60 seconds, pausing to scrape down once with a spatula).

3 Divide the dough in half. Pat one half into an even layer in the prepared pan. Set the other half aside. Bake for 20 to 25 minutes, until golden and crisp. Transfer to a rack and cool for 20 minutes. Leave the oven on.

4 Make the filling. Empty the jam into a medium bowl and stir well to break up any lumps. Add the cherries and stir until well mixed and all the cherries are coated with jam. Spread evenly over the cooled crust, all the way to the edges. Sprinkle the remaining dough evenly over the filling.

5 Bake for 35 to 40 minutes, until the topping is golden brown and the filling is bubbling. Transfer to a rack and cool completely, 1½ to 2 hours.

6 To serve, run a thin knife or spatula around the edges of the pan to loosen any dough or filling. Lift the cookies out using the foil as handles and place on a cutting surface. Cut into 3 by 1-inch bars. Just before serving, use the fine-mesh strainer to lightly dust the confectioners' sugar over the cookies.

Cupcakes

Classic Yellow Cupcakes
with Cream Cheese Frosting

MAKES 12 CUPCAKES

This buttery, vanilla-scented cake is a variation on a pound cake, with a little extra leavener added to lighten the crumb. Nearly any frosting pairs well with this celebration favorite. For a special party or tea, make the mini cupcakes variation at the end of the recipe (shown at left), then top them with swirls of Cream Cheese Frosting and finish them with pretty Sugared Flowers and/or touches of gold leaf.

1 Preheat the oven to 350°F and position an oven rack in the center. Line a standard-sized cupcake pan with 12 paper liners.

2 Make the cake. Place the butter and sugar in the bowl of a stand mixer and beat on medium until very light—almost white—in color, 4 to 5 minutes. You can also use a hand mixer and a medium bowl, although you may need to beat the mixture a little longer to achieve the same results. Scrape down the bowl with a spatula.

3 Beat the eggs and vanilla in a small bowl to blend. With the mixer on medium, add the eggs to the butter mixture about 1 tablespoon at a time, allowing each addition to completely blend in before adding the next. About halfway through, turn off the mixer and scrape down the bowl, then resume adding the eggs. Scrape down the bowl again.

. . . .

Ingredients

Cake

¾ cup (1½ sticks) unsalted butter, softened

¾ cup sugar

3 large eggs, at room temperature

1 tablespoon pure vanilla extract

2 cups sifted cake flour

¾ teaspoon baking soda

¼ teaspoon salt

⅓ cup sour cream, at room temperature

Cream Cheese Frosting

12 ounces cream cheese, at room temperature

6 tablespoons (¾ stick) unsalted butter, at room temperature

Finely grated zest of 1 lemon

3 cups unsifted confectioners' sugar

1½ teaspoons pure vanilla extract

. . . .

4 With the fine-mesh strainer, sift the cake flour, baking soda, and salt into a medium bowl and whisk together. With the mixer on the lowest speed, add the flour mixture and the sour cream alternately, beginning with one-third of the flour mixture and half the sour cream; repeat, then finish with the flour mixture. Scrape down the bowl and finish blending the batter by hand, if necessary.

5 Scrape the batter into the prepared cupcake pan, filling each cup to ¼ inch from the top of the liner. Bake for 15 to 20 minutes, until firm to the touch and a toothpick inserted into the center comes out clean. Transfer the pans to a wire rack and allow to cool completely.

6 Make the frosting. Place the cream cheese, butter, and lemon zest in the bowl of a stand mixer and blend on medium speed until smooth, about 1 minute. You can also use a hand mixer and a medium bowl, although you may need to beat the mixture a little longer to achieve the same results. Scrape down the bowl with a spatula and beat again for 15 seconds.

7 Use a fine-mesh strainer to sift in the confectioners' sugar and blend on low for 15 seconds, then scrape down the bowl. Add the vanilla, turn the speed to medium, and beat for 1 minute. Use immediately or refrigerate until needed.

8 Frost the cupcakes. Using a small offset spatula, evenly distribute the frosting among the cupcakes. These can be stored at room temperature for 2 days or in the refrigerator for up to 4 days. Be sure to remove from the refrigerator at least 1 hour before serving to allow the cake and frosting to soften to the perfect eating consistency.

Variation: Mini Yellow Cupcakes Bake the batter in mini muffin tins lined with mini cupcake liners. Fill each cup with 1 tablespoon of batter to ¼ inch from the top of the liner. Bake for 11 to 14 minutes until firm to the touch and a toothpick inserted into the center comes out clean. Makes about 50 mini cupcakes.

Gold Leaf: Gold or silver leaf comes in small square packets with tissue-thin square sheets of gold or silver tucked between sheets of paper. Be careful when opening the packet, as the leaves are so thin they will practically dissolve in the air if you fling it open and allow them to fall out of their sheaves. To apply gold or silver leaf, you'll need something for it to stick to—a moist line of melted chocolate, a tiny bit of frosting, even a tiny drop of water will help the leaf adhere to your dessert. Gently peel back one of the sheaves, exposing some of the leaf within. Hold the packet in one hand close to the dessert with a paring knife in the other hand. With the tip of the knife, pick up a piece of the gold or silver leaf, tear it off, and transfer it to the pastry, touching it to the point on the pastry where you want the gold or silver to stick. The little pieces of leaf are at their most beautiful when standing up, waving in the air slightly, catching the light. You can also gently smooth them down to lie flat with the knife tip or a small brush.

Sugared Flowers

• •

1 cup superfine sugar

1 to 2 tablespoons powdered pasteurized egg whites

Edible flowers (whole and/or petals)

• •

1   Line a baking sheet with parchment paper or a silicone mat. Pour the sugar onto a dinner plate and set aside. Place the powdered egg whites in a small bowl and add enough water to dilute them to the consistency of fresh egg whites. Mix gently with a small whisk or a fork until well blended (don't create froth).

2   Pick out the whole flowers and set them aside. Gently pull any petals you want to sugar off the remaining flowers. Make sure that both whole flowers and petals are clean and dry.

3   With a pair of tweezers, hold a flower or petal. Dip a small brush into the liquid egg whites and lightly paint the entire surface of the flower. You must cover every surface—front and back—with the whites, for any exposed surface will decompose. Hold the flower over the plate of sugar. Gently spoon the sugar over the flower, allowing the excess sugar to fall back onto the plate. Check both sides of the flower—if you missed a spot, simply touch it up with the brush and a little more sugar. Still holding the flower over the plate, gently tap the tweezers on the side of the plate (or with your finger) to knock off any excess sugar.

4   Set the flower on the prepared baking sheet and continue sugaring the remaining flowers and/or petals. When you have finished, go back through the sugared blooms and check again for any spots that may need touching up.

5   Set the baking sheet in a warm, dry place for several days, turning the flowers with the tweezers once a day to ensure that they dry evenly. This turning is especially important for whole flowers, as their heft and density can inhibit moisture from evaporating from the bottom of the flower. When the flowers are very dry, they will be crisp. Keep the sugared flowers between layers of parchment paper in an airtight container. If possible, set a small cup of desiccant in the container with the blooms (but don't let it touch the flowers) to absorb any excess moisture. Stored in a cool, dry location (not the refrigerator), the sugared flowers will keep for 2 to 3 months, and perhaps 6 months or more.

Ingredients

Cake

1 cup water

¾ cup buttermilk

¾ cup canola or corn oil

3 large eggs

2 cups unbleached all-purpose flour

1¾ cups sugar

¾ cup unsweetened natural cocoa powder

2 teaspoons baking soda

¼ teaspoon salt

Frosting

1¼ cups (2½ sticks) unsalted butter, softened

1¾ cups powdered sugar

1¼ cups creamy peanut butter (not natural style), at room temperature

To decorate

Reese's Pieces, cut-up peanut butter cups, or chocolate sprinkles (optional)

Chocolate-Peanut Butter

Cupcakes

MAKES 24 CUPCAKES

Peanut butter and chocolate is a classic, but irresistable combination. This frosting is so good, you might want to double the recipe to add a thicker layer on top these divine cupcakes.

1   Position 1 oven rack in the top third of the oven and 1 oven rack in the bottom third of the oven, and preheat the oven to 350°F. Line 2 standard-sized cupcake pans with 24 paper liners.

2   Make the cake. Put the water, buttermilk, oil, and eggs in a medium bowl. Whisk until the eggs have completely blended into the mixture.

3   Sift together the flour, sugar, cocoa powder, baking soda, and salt into a large bowl. Push through any lumps with your fingers.

4   Pour the liquid ingredients into the dry ingredients. Whisk gently at first, and then, as the mixture blends, whisk faster until you have a smooth batter and you don't see any more dry patches.

5   Using a silicone spatula, scrape the batter into the prepared cupcake pans, filling each cup no more than two-thirds full. Bake for 15 to 20 minutes, until a toothpick inserted into the center comes out clean. Let them cool completely on wire racks before frosting them.

6 Make the frosting. Place the softened butter in a large bowl. Sift half of the powdered sugar over the top of the butter. Using a stand mixer, beat on medium-low speed to blend it in thoroughly. Turn off the mixer and scrape down the sides of the bowl with a silicone spatula. Sift in the remaining powdered sugar and beat on medium-high speed for about 2 minutes, or until the mixture is blended and fluffy. Turn off the mixer and scrape down the sides of the bowl.

7 Add the peanut butter and beat on medium-high until blended and smooth. Scrape down the bowl one last time, and make sure there aren't any pockets of sugar or peanut butter hiding in the bottom of the bowl.

8 Frost the cupcakes. Divide the frosting evenly among the cupcake tops. There is enough frosting for about 2 level tablespoons on each cupcake. Using a small offset spatula, spread it all the way to the edges. These are delicious just like this. If you like, decorate the top with Reese's Pieces or anything you desire.

9 You can keep the cupcakes at room temperature for 2 days. After that, store any leftovers in the refrigerator. The frosting gets really hard in the fridge, so let the cupcakes sit at room temperature for at least 30 minutes before serving.

Ingredients

Chocolate Ganache

6 ounces semisweet or bittersweet chocolate (up to 60 percent cacao), finely chopped

¾ cup heavy whipping cream

Cake

¾ cup (1½ sticks) unsalted butter, softened

¾ cup sugar

4 large egg whites

1 tablespoon pure vanilla extract

2 cups sifted cake flour

¾ teaspoon baking soda

¼ teaspoon salt

⅓ cup sour cream, at room temperature ingredient

Classic White Cupcakes
with Chocolate Ganache

MAKES 12 CUPCAKES

Same delicious flavor, but with a soft white crumb that is especially appropriate for baby showers, weddings, and tea cakes. To use the ganache as a frosting, it should be prepared at least 8 hours ahead, covered, and stored at room temperature.

1 Make the ganache. Place the chocolate in a medium bowl. Heat the cream in a small saucepan over medium heat until it begins to boil. Immediately pour the cream over the chocolate. Let the mixture sit for 1 minute, then gently whisk until the ganache is completely smooth and blended. If you are using a high-percentage chocolate and the mixture looks broken or curdled at this point, stir in an extra tablespoon or two of cream, just until the mixture smooths out again.

2 To use as frosting: Let the ganache cool for 1 hour, then cover with plastic wrap and set aside to finish cooling at room temperature until it has the consistency of frosting, 8 to 10 hours. If you make it the night before, it will be the perfect texture for frosting cakes and cupcakes in the morning.

3 Preheat the oven to 350°F and position an oven rack in the center. Line a standard-sized cupcake pan with 12 paper liners.

4 Make the cake. Place the butter and sugar in the bowl of a stand mixer and beat on medium until very light—almost white—in color, 4 to 5 minutes. You can also use a hand mixer and a medium bowl, although you may need to beat the mixture a little longer to achieve the same results. Scrape down the bowl with a spatula.

5 Beat the egg whites and vanilla in a small bowl to blend. With the mixer on medium, add the eggs to the butter mixture about 1 tablespoon at a time, allowing each addition to completely blend in before adding the next. About halfway through, turn off the mixer and scrape down the bowl, then resume adding the eggs. Scrape down the bowl again.

6 With a fine-mesh strainer, sift the cake flour, baking soda, and salt into a medium bowl and whisk together. With the mixer on the lowest speed, add the flour mixture and the sour cream alternately, beginning with one-third of the flour mixture and half the sour cream; repeat, then finish with the flour mixture. Scrape down the bowl and finish blending the batter by hand, if necessary.

7 Scrape the batter into the prepared cupcake pan, filling each cup to ¼ inch from the top of the liner. Bake for 15 to 20 minutes, until firm to the touch and a toothpick inserted into the center comes out clean. Transfer the pan to a cooling rack to cool completely.

8 Frost the cupcakes. Use an offset spatula to evenly divide the chocolate ganache among the cupcakes. These can be stored at room temperature for 2 days or in the refrigerator for up to 4 days.

Rocky Road
Cupcakes

MAKES 20 CUPCAKES

These cupcakes are jam-packed with crunchy nuts, chewy marshmallows, rich chocolate, and a creamy marshmallow swirl. Are they more like ice cream or candy bars? You decide.

1   Preheat the oven to 350°F and position an oven rack in the center. Line 2 standard-sized cupcake pans with 20 paper liners.

2   Make the batter. Place the cocoa powder in a small bowl. Heat ½ cup of the water in a small saucepan just until it begins to simmer. Pour it over the cocoa and whisk until blended and smooth. Add the remaining 1 cup water and stir until the mixture is smooth. Set aside until the mixture cools to room temperature. If warm, it will melt the butter and ruin the texture of the cake.

3   Place the butter, granulated sugar, and brown sugar in the bowl of a stand mixer fitted with the paddle attachment and beat on medium speed until very light in color, 4 to 5 minutes. Scrape down the bowl with a spatula. With the mixer running on medium, add the eggs one at a time, pausing between each until incorporated. Add the vanilla and beat until combined.

Cake

½ cup unsifted unsweetened Dutch process cocoa powder

½ cup plus 1 cup water

¾ cup (1½ sticks) unsalted butter, softened

1 cup granulated sugar

¾ cup firmly packed light brown sugar

3 large eggs, at room temperature

2 teaspoons pure vanilla extract

2 cups sifted cake flour

¼ cup unbleached all-purpose flour

2 teaspoons baking powder

¼ teaspoon salt

Topping

¾ cup heavy cream

1 cup semisweet chocolate morsels

2 tablespoons (¼ stick) unsalted butter, at room temperature

2 teaspoons light corn syrup

1½ cups toasted walnut pieces

1 cup miniature marshmallows

¼ cup prepared marshmallow cream

Filling

1 cup prepared marshmallow cream

. . . .

4 With a fine-mesh strainer, sift the cake flour, all-purpose flour, baking powder, and salt into a medium bowl and blend with a whisk. With the mixer running on the lowest speed, add the flour mixture and the cocoa water alternately, beginning with one-third of the flour mixture and half of the cocoa water. Repeat, then finish with the flour mixture. Scrape down the bowl and finish blending the batter by hand, if necessary.

5 Divide the batter among the prepared cupcake pans and bake for 15 to 20 minutes, until the tops are firm to the touch and a toothpick inserted into the center comes out clean. Remove from the oven and allow to cool completely in the pans.

6 Make the topping. Scald the cream in a small saucepan over medium heat and pour over the chocolate morsels that have been placed in a medium bowl. Allow to rest for 5 minutes before stirring with a rubber spatula to combine. Add the softened butter and corn syrup, and mix thoroughly. The mixture needs to thicken to a frosting consistency. This can either be done the day before and stored covered at room temperature, or to proceed right away, the mixture can be placed in the refrigerator. The mixture should be stirred every 20 minutes until it has thickened to a frosting consistency. This will take approximately 2 hours.

7 Spread the nuts on a parchment-lined cookie sheet and bake in a 350°F oven for 10 to 12 minutes, until lightly toasted and fragrant. Remove the nuts from the oven and set aside to cool completely. Using a rubber spatula, stir the marshmallows and cooled nut pieces into the thickened topping, then gently fold in ¼ cup of marshmallow cream, creating a swirl. Do not overmix.

8 Fill the cupcakes. Using a small serrated paring knife, remove a 1½-inch diameter cone-shaped plug from the top of each cupcake and set it aside, making sure not to cut all the way through to the bottom of the cupcake. Evenly distribute the remaining 1 cup of marshmallow cream among the cupcakes and replace the cake plugs, gently pressing down and allowing the plug to sit up a little higher than the top of the cupcake.

9 Finish the cupcakes. Using a tablespoon, evenly distribute the topping among the filled cupcakes. These should be stored in a covered container at room temperature for up to 2 days.

Tiramisù
Cupcakes

MAKES 24 CUPCAKES

In Italian, tiramisù loosely means "pick-me-up" and these coffee-imbibed cupcakes will certainly give you a lift! Based on the traditional dessert, this portable version, with its creamy mascarpone topping, is reminiscent of the original.

1   Preheat the oven to 350°F and position an oven rack in the center. Line 2 standard-sized cupcake pans with 24 paper liners.

2   Make the coffee syrup. Combine the coffee and sugar in a small saucepan and bring to a boil, stirring with a whisk until the sugar is completely dissolved. Remove from the heat, whisk in the rum, and set aside.

3   Make the cake. Put the egg whites and the cream of tartar in the bowl of a stand mixer fitted with the whisk attachment. Whisk on medium speed until foamy, 1 to 2 minutes, then gradually add ½ cup of the sugar, raise the speed to high, and continue mixing until the whites are stiff and glossy. Using a rubber spatula, gently transfer the egg whites to another bowl and set aside.

4   In a medium bowl, combine the sugar, flour, baking powder, and salt with a whisk and set aside. Put the egg yolks, oil, milk, and vanilla in a clean bowl of a stand mixer. Using the whisk

Coffee Syrup
¾ cup strong brewed coffee
⅓ cup sugar
¼ cup dark rum

Cake
7 large eggs, separated
¼ teaspoon cream of tartar
1½ cups sugar
2 cups unbleached all-purpose flour
2½ teaspoons baking powder
½ teaspoon salt
½ cup vegetable oil
¾ cup whole milk
1 tablespoon pure vanilla extract

Mascarpone Topping
1½ cups mascarpone cheese
1 cup heavy cream
¼ cup sugar
1 teaspoon vanilla extract
Cocoa powder for decoration
....

attachment, mix on medium speed for 3 to 4 minutes, until pale yellow. With the mixer running on low speed, gradually add the flour mixture and mix to combine, scraping down the sides of the bowl as necessary. Using a rubber spatula, transfer the mixture to a large bowl and fold in the egg whites, starting with a third until just incorporated, then adding another third and folding until just incorporated, then finishing with the final third, being careful not to overmix.

5   Divide the batter evenly among the 24 liners and bake for 20 to 24 minutes, until the tops are golden brown. Remove from the oven and, using a thin wooden skewer, poke 12 holes in each cupcake approximately three-quarters of the way down. Using a small pastry brush, apply the coffee syrup to the tops of the cupcakes, being sure to distribute all of the syrup evenly. Transfer the pans to a wire rack and allow to cool completely.

6   Make the topping. Put the mascarpone cheese in the bowl of a stand mixer fitted with the whisk attachment and beat on medium speed while drizzling in the cream, until combined. Add the sugar and vanilla all at once and whisk until stiff peaks form, 1 to 2 minutes, being careful not to overwhip.

7   Remove the cupcakes from the pans and place on a plate or platter. Using a rubber spatula, transfer the topping to a large pastry bag fitted with a ½-inch round metal tip. In a circular motion, evenly pipe the topping among the cupcake tops. Using a small fine-mesh sifter, dust the tops of each cupcake with the cocoa powder. The cupcakes should be stored lightly covered with plastic wrap in the refrigerator for up to 2 days. Allow to come to room temperature for 30 minutes before serving.

Pumpkin Spice Cupcakes

with Maple–Cream Cheese Frosting

MAKES 18 CUPCAKES

When the leaves are falling and the air is crisp, these cupcakes will warm the kitchen with the fragrance of fall. The comforting flavor of spiced pumpkin in a soft and tender cake is layered with a luscious cream cheese frosting sweetened with real maple syrup. Be sure to use the darkest, most flavorful maple syrup you can find—look for Grade C, which is not an indication of quality but of darkness and intensity of flavor. School party? Top each one with a little candy pumpkin.

1   Preheat the oven to 350°F and position the oven racks in the upper and lower thirds of the oven. Line 2 standard-sized cupcake tins with 18 paper liners.

2   Make the cake. Beat the butter and brown sugar in the bowl of a stand mixer on medium-high until very light in color, 4 to 5 minutes. You can also use a hand mixer and a medium bowl, although you may need to beat the mixture a little longer to achieve the same results. Scrape down the bowl with a spatula.

3   Beat the eggs and vanilla in a small bowl to blend. With the mixer on medium, add the eggs to the butter mixture about 1 tablespoon at a time, allowing each addition to completely blend in before adding the next. About halfway through, turn off the mixer and scrape down the bowl, then resume adding the eggs. Scrape down the bowl again. Add the pumpkin and blend well.

Ingredients

Cake

½ cup (1 stick) unsalted butter, softened

1½ cups firmly packed light brown sugar

2 large eggs, at room temperature

1 teaspoon pure vanilla extract

1 cup canned pumpkin puree (not spiced pumpkin pie filling)

2 cups sifted cake flour

1 teaspoon baking soda

¼ teaspoon baking powder

¼ teaspoon salt

½ teaspoon ground cinnamon

¼ teaspoon ground allspice

¼ teaspoon ground nutmeg

⅛ teaspoon ground cloves

½ cup buttermilk, at room temperature

Frosting

12 ounces cream cheese, at room temperature

6 tablespoons (¾ stick) unsalted butter, at room temperature

½ cup plus 1 tablespoon pure maple syrup, preferably Grade C

1¾ cups sifted confectioners' sugar

1 cup pecan pieces, toasted and finely chopped, for garnish

4   With the fine-mesh strainer, sift the cake flour, baking soda, baking powder, salt, cinnamon, allspice, nutmeg, and cloves into a medium bowl and whisk to blend. With the mixer on the lowest speed, add the flour mixture and the buttermilk alternately, beginning with one-third of the flour mixture and half of the buttermilk; repeat, then finish with the flour mixture. Scrape down the bowl and finish blending the batter by hand.

5   Fill each liner three-fourths full with batter. Bake for 15 to 20 minutes, until the tops are firm to the touch and a toothpick inserted into the centers comes out clean. Cool the cupcakes completely on a cooling rack. Frost the cupcakes the day you wish to serve them.

6   Make the frosting: Place the cream cheese and butter in the bowl of a mixer or a food processor. Blend until smooth. Add the maple syrup and confectioners' sugar and mix thoroughly. Scrape down the bowl with a clean spatula and blend again briefly.

7   Frost the cupcakes. Using a small offset spatula, evenly distribute the frosting among the cupcakes, being sure the frosting covers the entire top. Garnish with the nuts. These should be stored in the refrigerator for up to 3 days. Be sure to take them out of the refrigerator 30 minutes before serving.

Raspberry Cupcakes
with Key Lime Frosting

MAKES 20 CUPCAKES

Light and bursting with fresh raspberry flavor, these cupcakes will be a favorite for your summer gatherings. The Key lime adds just the right amount of contrast to the berries. Other fresh seasonal berries may be substituted or combined.

1   Preheat the oven to 350°F and position an oven rack in the center. Line 2 standard-sized cupcake pans with 20 paper liners.

2   Make the batter. Put the butter and granulated sugar in the bowl of a stand mixer fitted with the paddle attachment and cream on medium speed for 2 to 3 minutes, occasionally scraping down the sides with a rubber spatula, until light and fluffy. With the mixer running on low speed, add the eggs (plus the additional white) one at a time until they are fully incorporated. Add the vanilla and mix to combine.

3   In a medium bowl, combine the flour, baking powder, and salt with a whisk and set aside. With the mixer running on low speed, add a third of the flour mixture; when combined, add half of the milk, mixing until just blended. Repeat with the second third of the flour mixture and the remaining milk, mixing until just blended, and add the final third of the flour mixture and mix until just combined. Put the raspberries in a medium

Ingredients

Cake

1 cup (2 sticks) salted butter, at room temperature

2 cups granulated sugar

3 large eggs, plus 1 egg white

2 teaspoons pure vanilla extract

3 cups unbleached all-purpose flour

1 tablespoon baking powder

1 teaspoon salt

1 cup whole milk

1 cup fresh raspberries, slightly mashed

Frosting

½ cup (1 stick) salted butter, at room temperature

8 ounces cream cheese, at room temperature

1 tablespoon Key lime zest

2 tablespoons Key lime juice

5 cups powdered sugar, sifted

bowl and slightly mash with a fork. Using a rubber spatula, fold the raspberries into the batter just to combine. Do not overmix.

4   Divide the batter evenly among the lined cupcake pans and bake for 20 to 24 minutes, until light golden brown. Remove from the oven and allow to cool in the pans on a rack. When cool, remove the cupcakes from the pans and set aside.

5   Make the frosting. Put the butter and cream cheese in the bowl of a stand mixer fitted with the paddle attachment and mix on medium speed until evenly combined, scraping down the sides of the bowl as necessary. Turn the speed down to low and add the lime zest and juice, mixing until combined. While the machine is running, slowly add the powdered sugar, using a large spoon, until thoroughly combined. Increase the speed to medium and mix until light and fluffy, 3 to 4 minutes.

6   Frost the cupcakes. Using a small offset spatula, evenly distribute the frosting among the cupcakes, making sure the frosting covers the entire top. These should be stored lightly covered in the refrigerator for up to 2 days. Allow to come to room temperature for 30 minutes before serving.

Variation: Mini Raspberry Cupcakes with Key Lime Frosting Prepare the oven as directed for the standard-sized cupcakes. Line the cups of mini cupcake tins with mini cupcake liners, filling each one with 1 rounded tablespoon of batter to ¼ inch from the top of the liner. Bake for 12 to 15 minutes, until light golden brown. Remove from the oven and allow to cool in the pans on a rack. When cool, remove the cupcakes from the pans and frost as directed. Makes approximately 90 mini cupcakes.

Ingredients

Cake

1 cup seedless raisins

¼ cup dark rum

½ cup (1 stick) salted butter, at room temperature

1¾ cups granulated sugar

3 large eggs, separated

1½ cups sifted cake flour

¾ teaspoon baking soda

¼ teaspoon salt

⅔ cup buttermilk

1 cup sweetened flaked coconut

¼ teaspoon cream of tartar

Frosting

1 cup flaked sweetened coconut

1 cup (2 sticks) salted butter, at room temperature

5 cups powdered sugar, sifted

¼ cup whole milk

2 teaspoons pure vanilla extract

Coconut Rum Raisin

Cupcakes

MAKES 20 CUPCAKES

The heady combination of rum, raisins, and toasted coconut in these cupcakes is definitely geared for the adult set. However, substituting orange or pineapple juice for the rum makes them kid friendly.

1   Preheat the oven to 350°F and position an oven rack in the center. Line 2 standard-sized cupcake pans with 20 paper liners.

2   In a small saucepan, combine the raisins and rum over low heat until warmed through. Do not boil. Turn off the heat and allow to cool to room temperature.

3   Make the batter. Put the butter and 1½ cups granulated sugar in the bowl of a stand mixer fitted with the paddle attachment and cream on medium speed for 2 to 3 minutes, scraping down the bowl as necessary. With the mixer running on low speed, add the egg yolks one at a time, pausing between each addition until combined.

4   In a medium bowl, combine the flour, baking soda, and salt with a whisk and set aside. With the mixer running on low speed, add a third of the flour mixture; when combined, add half of the buttermilk, mixing until just blended. Repeat with the second third of the flour mixture and the remaining buttermilk,

mixing until just blended; add the final third of the flour mixture and mix until just combined. Place the batter in a large bowl and with a rubber spatula stir in the rum-soaked raisins (with any remaining rum) and the coconut and set aside.

5   Put the egg whites and the cream of tartar in a clean bowl of a stand mixer fitted with the whisk attachment and mix on medium speed until foamy. Slowly add the remaining ¼ cup sugar until fully incorporated. Switch the machine to high speed and mix until the egg whites form stiff glossy peaks, 3 to 4 minutes. Using a rubber spatula, gently fold the egg whites into the batter in three separate additions, being careful not to overmix.

6   Divide the batter among the prepared cupcake pans and bake for 20 to 24 minutes, until the cupcakes are a light golden brown. Remove from the oven and allow to cool completely in the pans on a wire rack.

7   Make the frosting. Thinly spread the coconut onto a parchment-lined cookie sheet and bake in a 350°F oven until golden, stirring occasionally for even browning. Remove the coconut from the oven and set aside to cool completely. Put the butter in the bowl of a stand mixer fitted with the paddle attachment and mix on low speed while slowly adding the powdered sugar, scraping down the sides of the bowl as necessary. Drizzle in the milk and vanilla until combined. Increase the speed to medium and mix until light and fluffy, 3 to 4 minutes.

8   Frost the cupcakes. Using a small offset spatula, evenly distribute the frosting among the cupcakes, being sure the frosting covers the entire top. Immediately sprinkle on the toasted coconut. These should be stored in a covered container at room temperature for up to 2 days.

Ingredients

Crust

1 cup graham cracker crumbs

½ teaspoon cinnamon

2 tablespoons (¼ stick) butter, melted

Cheesecake

3 (8-ounce) packages cream cheese, at room temperature

1⅓ cups sugar

3 large eggs, at room temperature

¼ cup fresh lemon juice

1 teaspoon vanilla extract

Zest of 1 medium lemon

Glaze

¾ cup water

⅓ cup fresh lemon juice

1 egg yolk

½ cup sugar

1½ tablespoons cornstarch

¼ teaspoon salt

1 tablespoon butter

Zest of 1 medium lemon

. . . .

Lemon Cheesecake Cupcakes
with Lemon Glaze

MAKES 16 CUPCAKES

Freshly squeezed lemon juice and a hint of cinnamon transform ordinary cheesecake into an extraordinary dessert—the grated lemon zest gives it an extra punch! Try experimenting with different citrus juices and zest to create your own signature dessert.

1   Preheat the oven to 350°F and position an oven rack in the center. Line 2 standard-sized cupcake pans with 16 paper liners.

2   Make the crust. In a small bowl, combine the graham cracker crumbs and the ground cinnamon. Pour in the melted butter and stir to incorporate. Using a tablespoon, evenly distribute the crust among the 16 liners, pressing gently into the bottom using your fingers. Bake for 5 minutes. Remove from the oven and allow to cool.

3   Make the cheesecake filling. Put the cream cheese and sugar in the metal bowl of a stand mixer fitted with the paddle attachment and cream on medium speed for 2 to 3 minutes, occasionally scraping down the sides with a rubber spatula. With the mixer running on low speed, add the eggs one at a time, pausing between each until incorporated. Scrape the

sides of the bowl with a rubber spatula as needed. Turn off the mixer and add the lemon juice, vanilla, and lemon zest. Mix on low speed until combined. Divide the batter evenly among the 16 liners. Bake for 18 to 20 minutes, until slightly puffed in the center. Remove from the oven and allow to cool completely on a wire rack. It is normal for the cakes to settle in the center when cooling. When cool, remove the cupcakes from the pans, place on a plate or platter, and refrigerate for 1 hour.

4   Make the glaze. Place the water, lemon juice, and egg yolk in a small saucepan and combine with a whisk. Add the sugar, cornstarch, and salt and whisk to combine. Cook the mixture over medium heat, whisking constantly, until it has thickened and becomes somewhat translucent, about 4 to 5 minutes. Remove from the heat, whisk in the butter and lemon zest, and transfer to a small bowl to cool. To prevent a skin from forming, place plastic wrap directly on the surface of the curd.

5   Assemble the cakes. Divide the cooled lemon glaze evenly on top of the cheesecakes. The cheesecakes should be stored lightly covered in plastic wrap in the refrigerator. Allow to come to room temperature for 30 minutes before serving.

Ingredients

Cake

16 small chocolate peppermint patty candies

1 cup unbleached all-purpose flour

1 cup unsweetened cocoa powder

1 teaspoon salt

½ teaspoon baking powder

1 cup (2 sticks) unsalted butter

1½ cups granulated sugar

2 teaspoons instant espresso (dissolved in 2 tablespoons hot water)

4 large eggs, lightly beaten

1 tablespoon pure vanilla extract

Mint Ganache

⅓ cup heavy cream

½ cup semisweet chocolate morsels

1 tablespoon unsalted butter, at room temperature

1 teaspoon light corn syrup

½ teaspoon peppermint oil

Flat Icing

½ cup powdered sugar, sifted

1 tablespoon warm water

Chocolate Mint
Cupcakes

MAKES 16 CUPCAKES

This rich chocolate brownie-like cupcake hides a peppermint patty surprise inside! The "cool sensation" is enhanced with the silky finish of the striped mint ganache. Use peppermint oil instead of extract for a true mint flavor.

1   Preheat the oven to 350°F and position an oven rack in the center. Line 2 standard-sized cupcake pans with 16 paper liners. Unwrap the peppermint patty candies and keep chilled.

2   Make the cake. Using a fine-mesh strainer, sift together the flour, cocoa powder, salt, and baking powder in a medium bowl and set aside.

3   Place the butter in a small saucepan and melt completely over very low heat. Pour the butter into a medium bowl, add the granulated sugar, and using a rubber spatula mix to combine. Stir in the dissolved espresso, eggs, and vanilla. Stir in the flour mixture, being careful not to overmix.

4   Fill each liner a quarter full with batter. Place 1 chilled candy in each liner. Evenly distribute the remaining batter among the 16 liners.

5   Bake for 15 to 20 minutes, until the batter is set. Transfer to a cooling rack to cool completely.

6 Make the ganache. Scald the cream in a small saucepan over medium heat and pour over the chocolate morsels that have been placed in a medium bowl. Allow to rest for 5 minutes before stirring with a rubber spatula to combine. Add the softened butter, corn syrup, and peppermint oil and mix thoroughly.

7 Invert each cupcake and dip into the ganache, allowing the excess to run off. Place the cupcakes on a piece of parchment paper. The edges should not touch.

8 Glaze the cupcakes. While the ganache is setting up, combine the powdered sugar and water in a small bowl, mixing until smooth. Using a fork, lightly drizzle the icing over the cupcakes to make thin lines. You can adjust the icing by adding small amounts of water or sugar until it runs freely.

Ingredients

Cake

½ cup (1 stick) salted butter, at room temperature

2 cups sugar

6 tablespoons vegetable oil

6 large eggs, at room temperature

2 teaspoons pure vanilla extract

2½ cups unbleached all-purpose flour

1 tablespoon plus 1 teaspoon baking powder

½ cup cornstarch

½ teaspoon salt

1 cup whole milk

Custard Filling

2¼ cups whole milk

½ cup sugar

¼ cup cornstarch

5 egg yolks

1 tablespoon salted butter, cold

2 teaspoons vanilla extract

Glaze

¾ cup heavy cream

1 cup semisweet chocolate morsels

1 tablespoon salted butter, at room temperature

1 tablespoon light corn syrup

Boston Cream
Cupcakes

MAKES 24 CUPCAKES

Created by French chef M. Sanzian at Boston's Parker House Hotel, Boston cream pie was once considered a pie because it was baked in a pie tin due to the unavailability of cake pans. Here's a pint-sized take on the Massachusetts state dessert.

1   Preheat the oven to 350°F and position an oven rack in the center. Lightly butter 2 standard-sized cupcake pans or spray with pan spray.

2   Make the batter. Put the butter and sugar in the bowl of a stand mixer fitted with the paddle attachment and cream on medium speed for 2 to 3 minutes, occasionally scraping down the sides with a rubber spatula. While the mixer is running on low speed, drizzle in the oil, scraping down the sides as necessary. Turn the mixer to medium speed and mix for 1 to 2 minutes, until the mixture is light and fluffy.

3   With the mixer running on low speed, add the eggs one at a time until they are fully incorporated. Add the vanilla.

4   In a medium bowl, combine the flour, baking powder, cornstarch, and salt with a whisk. Set aside.

5   With the mixer running on low speed, add a third of the flour mixture; when combined, add half the milk, mixing until just

blended. Repeat with the second third of the flour mixture and the remaining milk, mixing until just blended; add the final third of the flour mixture and mix until just combined.

6   Divide the batter among the prepared cupcake pans and bake for 15 to 20 minutes, until the cupcakes are light golden brown. Remove from the oven and allow to cool in the pans on a rack. When cool, remove the cupcakes from the pans and set aside. If the cupcakes do not release easily, carefully go around the sides of the cupcakes with a small offset spatula.

7   Make the custard filling. In a medium saucepan, scald the milk and set aside. In a medium bowl, combine the sugar and cornstarch with a whisk. Add the yolks all at once and whisk together until light in color, about 1 minute. Slowly pour half the scalded milk into the sugar mixture, whisking constantly until combined; pour into the saucepan with the remaining milk. Cook the mixture over medium heat, whisking constantly, until thickened, 3 to 5 minutes. Remove from the heat and whisk in the cold butter and vanilla. Pour the custard into a medium glass or stainless-steel bowl and cover with plastic wrap placed directly on the surface of the custard to help prevent a skin from forming. Refrigerate until completely chilled.

8   Make the glaze. Scald the cream in a small saucepan over medium heat and pour over the chocolate morsels that have been placed in a medium bowl. Allow to rest for 5 minutes before stirring with a rubber spatula to combine. Add the softened butter and corn syrup and mix thoroughly.

9   Assemble the cupcakes. Using a small serrated knife, cut all the cupcakes in half horizontally, placing each cupcake top to the side of the bottom. Take the custard from the refrigerator and remove the plastic wrap. Whisk the custard for approximately 1 minute. Evenly divide the custard among the 24 cupcake bottoms, placing the tops on the custard. Transfer the filled cupcakes to a parchment-lined cookie sheet.

10 Glaze the cupcakes. Using a tablespoon, cover the top of each cupcake with the glaze, allowing some to drip down the sides. Transfer the cupcakes to the refrigerator until the glaze has set, approximately 15 minutes. Serve or lightly cover in plastic wrap and return to the refrigerator to store.

Ingredients

Pan Spread

3 tablespoons salted butter

1 cup light brown sugar, packed

1 (20-ounce) can crushed pineapple, drained

14 maraschino cherries, stems removed

Cake

¼ cup (½ stick) salted butter, at room temperature

1 cup granulated sugar

3 tablespoons vegetable oil

3 large eggs, at room temperature

1¼ cups unbleached all-purpose flour

¼ cup cornstarch

2 teaspoons baking powder

½ cup whole milk

1 tablespoon dark rum

Pineapple Upside-Down
Cupcakes

MAKES 14 CUPCAKES

Evoking the spirit of the islands, this is a classic dessert in miniature form! Buttery cake with a brown sugar and pineapple topping will be sure to please young and old alike. Chopped pecans may be substituted for the cherries for a delightful crunch.

1   Preheat the oven to 350°F and position an oven rack in the center.

2   Prepare the pans with the spread. Melt the butter in a small microwaveable bowl for approximately 25 seconds, or until melted. Using a small pastry brush, distribute the butter evenly among each cupcake tin, being sure to coat it completely. Some of the butter will pool in the bottom of the tin; this is okay. Evenly divide the brown sugar and then the pineapple among the buttered tins. Place a cherry in the center of each tin, slightly pushing down toward the bottom of the tin.

3   Make the batter. Put the butter and granulated sugar in the bowl of a stand mixer fitted with the paddle attachment and cream on medium speed for 2 to 3 minutes, scraping down the bowl as necessary. Drizzle in the oil and continue mixing until combined. Add the eggs one at a time, pausing between each addition until combined. In a medium bowl, combine the flour, cornstarch, and baking powder with a whisk and set aside.

Combine the milk and rum in a measuring cup and set aside. With the mixer running on low speed, add a third of the flour mixture; when combined, add half of the milk, mixing until just blended. Repeat with the second third of the flour mixture and the remaining milk, mixing until just blended; add the final third of the flour mixture and mix until just combined.

4   Divide the batter among the prepared cupcake pans and bake for 15 to 20 minutes, until the cupcakes are a light golden brown. Remove from the oven and allow to cool on a rack for 5 minutes. Carefully go around the sides of the cupcakes with a small offset spatula, invert the pan onto a parchment-lined cookie sheet, and tap a few times to help release the cupcakes. Carefully lift the pan and either serve immediately or allow the cupcakes to cool completely. These should be stored in a covered container at room temperature.

Whoopie Pies

Strawberry and Lemonade
Whoopie Pies

MAKES ABOUT 24 ASSEMBLED PIES

These whoopie pies are pretty enough for a princess party and delicious enough for a family picnic. You may find it difficult to decide what you like best—the soft pink color of these pies or the tart lemonade filling sandwiched between two strawberry cakes. A sprinkling of lemon zest on the outside is magical.

1   Preheat the oven to 375°F and position an oven rack in the center. Lay 1 nonstick silicone baking mat or a piece of parchment on each baking sheet.

2   Make the cake. In a medium mixing bowl, mix the flour, baking powder, and salt together. Set aside.

3   Cream the butter with the shortening in the bowl of a stand mixer fitted with the paddle attachment on low speed until completely mixed. Scrape the sides of the bowl well with a rubber spatula. Add the sugar and continue mixing on medium for 3 minutes, until the mixture is fluffy. Add the eggs a little at a time and mix until incorporated, about 3 to 4 minutes. Scrape the sides of the bowl again.

4   Mix the vanilla, milk, and strawberry powder, if using. (If you prefer more pink color, add up to ¼ teaspoon strawberry flavor powdered drink mix to the milk before you add it to the batter.) Turn the mixer on low and begin adding half the flour and

Cake

2½ cups unbleached all-purpose flour

2½ teaspoons baking powder

½ teaspoon salt

½ cup (1 stick) unsalted butter, at room temperature

¼ cup vegetable shortening

1½ cups granulated sugar

2 eggs, lightly beaten

½ teaspoon pure vanilla extract

⅓ cup milk

¼ teaspoon strawberry flavor powdered drink mix (optional)

6 ounces (about 12 whole) frozen strawberries, thawed and drained

Filling

1½ cups vegetable shortening

1¼ cups marshmallow cream

1 cup powdered sugar

¼ teaspoon lemon oil

1 teaspoon lemon juice

1 package (.23 ounce) lemonade flavored powdered drink mix (optional)

....

half the milk in alternating batches. Repeat with the remaining portions and turn the mixer off as soon as all the ingredients are mixed.

5   Drain any liquid from the thawed strawberries. In the bowl of a food processor fitted with the blade attachment, puree the strawberries to a fine puree. Pour the puree into the batter and mix by hand until incorporated.

6   Scoop the batter into tablespoon-sized balls using a spring-loaded cookie scoop or a spoon and place about 2 inches apart on the prepared baking sheet. Bake the cakes one sheet at a time for 11 to 13 minutes, until they are puffed. Transfer to a cooling rack and let cool completely. The cakes will fall somewhat as they cool.

7   Make the filling. Place the shortening and marshmallow cream in the bowl of a stand mixer fitted with the paddle attachment. Cream them together on medium speed for 4 minutes. Use a rubber spatula to scrape the sides of the bowl. Place the powdered sugar in the bowl, starting on low speed to incorporate the powdered sugar. Then increase the speed to medium and beat for an additional 4 minutes. Add the lemon oil and lemon juice and mix an additional minute. For a true lemonade flavor, add a package of lemonade-flavored drink mix and beat an additional minute, if desired.

8   Assemble and fill the pies. Transfer the filling to a pastry bag fitted with a number 10 (or larger) pastry tip. Pipe the filling on the flat side of half of the cakes. If you don't have a pastry bag, you can spread the filling with a knife or offset spatula. Match cakes that are closest in size and place the second cake on top so that the filling is sandwiched between two flat sides. Store the assembled whoopie pies in a plastic container with a cookie rack fitted inside to prevent sticking. However, they are best eaten within 24 hours.

Alternate Baking Method: Use greased whoopie pie pans. Place 1½ tablespoons of batter into each cavity. Do not overfill the pans or your whoopie cakes will dome in the center.

Bake in a 375°F oven for 10 to 12 minutes. Turn the cakes out onto a wire rack and cool completely before filling. Proceed with filling and assembling as directed.

Tips for Freezing: If you need to make the cakes ahead of time, first bake and cool them completely. Then put them in layers in a plastic container, placing wax paper or parchment between the layers. They will keep for 2 weeks in the freezer.

To defrost the cakes, uncover them and lay them flat in a single layer on baking sheets. Let them come to room temperature, about 3 to 4 hours, before filling. The filling should be made the day you plan to use it. Proceed with filling the cakes as directed.

Oatmeal Raisin with Orange Cream Cheese

Whoopie Pies

MAKES ABOUT 24 ASSEMBLED PIES

Whoopie pie purists may argue that this isn't a "real" whoopie pie since we've replaced the traditional marshmallow cream filling with cream cheese filling, but they may think twice after tasting just how delicious this version is.

1   Preheat the oven to 375°F and position an oven rack in the center. Lay 1 nonstick silicone baking mat or a piece of parchment on each baking sheet.

2   Make the cake. In a small saucepan, cook the oats in 1 cup water according to the package directions. Remove from the heat. Stir in the raisins and vanilla. Cover and let cool completely at room temperature.

3   In a medium mixing bowl, mix the flour, baking powder, baking soda, salt, and cinnamon together. Set aside.

4   Cream the butter with the shortening in the bowl of a stand mixer fitted with the paddle attachment on low speed until completely mixed. Scrape the sides of the bowl well with a rubber spatula. Add the granulated sugar and brown sugar, and continue mixing on high for 3 minutes, until the mixture is light brown. Add the eggs and mix until incorporated. Scrape the sides of the bowl well.

Ingredients

Cake

½ cup rolled oats

1 cup water

½ cup raisins

1 teaspoon vanilla extract

2 cups unbleached all-purpose flour

1 teaspoon baking powder

¼ teaspoon baking soda

½ teaspoon salt

1 teaspoon cinnamon

⅓ cup unsalted butter, at room temperature

⅓ cup vegetable shortening

½ cup granulated sugar

½ cup brown sugar, packed

2 eggs, lightly beaten

Filling

6 ounces cream cheese, at room temperature

½ cup (1 stick) unsalted butter, at room temperature

1¼ cups powdered sugar

½ teaspoon orange oil

5 Add the flour mixture, then turn the mixer on low and mix until incorporated. Remove the bowl from the stand and scrape the sides of the bowl well with a rubber spatula. Remove the paddle attachment and scrape any remaining batter into the bowl. Using the rubber spatula, stir the cooked and cooled oatmeal-raisin mixture into the batter. Stop stirring as soon as all the ingredients are blended.

6 Scoop the batter into tablespoon-sized balls using a spring-loaded cookie scoop or a spoon and place about 2 inches apart on the prepared baking sheet. Bake the cakes one sheet at a time for 12 to 15 minutes, until the cakes are puffed and your finger does not leave an indentation when the cakes are lightly touched. Transfer to a cooling rack and let cool completely.

7 Make the filling. Place the cream cheese in the bowl of a stand mixer fitted with the paddle attachment. Cream on medium speed for about a minute to completely soften the cream cheese. Scrape the sides of the bowl well with a rubber spatula. Add the butter and cream cheese together until completely incorporated, about 1 minute. Scrape the sides of the bowl again. Add the powdered sugar and orange oil to the bowl. Turn the mixer on low speed until the ingredients begin to come together. Increase the speed to medium and mix for 1 to 2 minutes, or until easily spreadable.

8 Assemble and fill the pies. Transfer the filling to a pastry bag fitted with a number 10 (or larger) pastry tip. Pipe the filling on the flat side of half of the cakes. If you don't have a pastry bag, you can spread the filling with a knife or offset spatula. Match cakes that are closest in size and place the second cake on top so that the filling is sandwiched between two flat sides. Store the assembled whoopie pies in a plastic container with a cookie rack fitted inside to prevent sticking. They are best eaten within 24 hours.

Alternate Baking Method: Use greased whoopie pie pans. Place 1½ tablespoons of batter into each cavity. Do not overfill the pans or your whoopie cakes will dome in the center.

Bake in a 375°F oven for 10 to 12 minutes. Turn the cakes out onto a wire rack and cool completely before filling. Proceed with filling and assembling as directed.

Tips for Freezing: See page 74.

Bananas Foster
Whoopie Pies

MAKES ABOUT 20 ASSEMBLED PIES

**Children will love being little helpers by peeling and mashing the
overripe bananas for this recipe. The traditional marshmallow cream
filling given as a variation is suitable for children, but adults will love
the sophisticated update these pies get from the rum-infused filling.
Either way, you'll probably have trouble keeping these around for long.**

1 Preheat the oven to 375°F and position an oven rack in
   the center. Lay 1 nonstick silicone baking mat or a piece of
   parchment on each baking sheet.

2 Make the cake. Make the almond sugar by placing the
   granulated sugar in a food processor. Add the almonds and
   grind together until the almonds are ground as finely as the
   sugar, about 1 minute.

3 Cream the shortening, butter, and almond sugar in the bowl
   of a stand mixer fitted with the paddle attachment on medium
   speed until completely mixed. Scrape the sides of the bowl well
   with a rubber spatula. Add the eggs and mix on medium speed
   for 2 to 3 minutes, until the mixture is smooth. Scrape the sides
   of the bowl well with the rubber spatula.

4 Mash the bananas with a fork in a small bowl, then transfer
   to a food processor. Puree until smooth. Sprinkle the baking
   soda on top of the banana puree. Pour the banana mixture

Cake

1 cup granulated sugar

¼ cup toasted sliced almonds

¼ cup vegetable shortening

¼ cup (½ stick) unsalted butter,
   at room temperature

2 eggs, lightly beaten

1 cup (about 2½ medium) pureed
   overripe bananas

1 teaspoon baking soda

½ teaspoon pure vanilla extract

2 cups unbleached all-purpose
   flour

Pinch of salt

½ teaspoon cinnamon

3 tablespoons milk

Filling

5 tablespoons brown sugar

2 tablespoons dark rum (such as
   Myers's Rum)

½ teaspoon cinnamon

1½ cups marshmallow cream

1¼ cups vegetable shortening

1 cup powdered sugar

into the medium mixing bowl with the sugar, shortening, egg mixture, and vanilla. Turn the mixer on medium and mix 2 to 3 minutes, until the banana mixture incorporates into the shortening mixture. At first it will appear broken, but be patient and it will smooth itself out. Scrape the sides of the bowl well with a rubber spatula.

5   In a medium mixing bowl, mix the flour, salt, and cinnamon. Blend with a fork to evenly distribute the dry ingredients.

6   Pour the dry ingredients into the banana mixture and mix on low speed. Add the milk. Stop mixing as soon as the ingredients have come together.

7   Scoop the batter into tablespoon-sized portions using a spring-loaded cookie scoop or a spoon and place about 2 inches apart on the prepared baking sheets. Using your finger, press down on each portion to level it out slightly. These cakes puff extremely well, and leveling them helps them achieve the perfect shape in the oven. Bake the cakes one sheet at a time for 11 to 13 minutes, until your finger does not leave an indentation in the cakes when touched lightly. Transfer to a cooling rack and let cool completely.

8   Make the filling. Place the brown sugar, rum, and cinnamon in a very small bowl or ramekin. Let this mixture sit so that the rum begins to melt the sugar. Meanwhile, put the marshmallow cream and shortening in a medium bowl of a stand mixer and mix on medium speed for 2 to 3 minutes with a paddle attachment. Use a rubber spatula to scrape the sides of the bowl. Place the powdered sugar in the bowl with the creamed mixture, add the brown sugar mixture, and mix on low speed until the ingredients begin to come together. Increase the speed to medium and mix for 2 to 3 minutes, until fluffy.

9   Assemble and fill the pies. Transfer the brown sugar filling into a pastry bag fitted with a number 10 (or larger) pastry tip. Pipe the filling on the flat side of half of the cakes. If you don't have a pastry bag, you can spread the filling with a knife or offset spatula. Match cakes that are closest in size and place the second cake on top so that the filling is sandwiched between two flat sides. Store the assembled whoopie pies in a plastic container with a cookie rack fitted inside to prevent sticking. They are best eaten within 24 hours.

Alternate Baking Method: Use greased whoopie pie pans. Place 1½ tablespoons of batter into each cavity. Do not overfill the pans or your whoopie cakes will dome in the center.

Bake in a 350°F oven for 11 to 13 minutes. Turn the cakes out onto a wire rack and cool completely before filling. Proceed with filling and assembling as directed.

Variation for traditional marshmallow cream filling

1½ cups marshmallow cream
1¼ cups vegetable shortening
1 cup powdered sugar
1 tablespoon vanilla extract

•••

Put the marshmallow cream and shortening in a medium bowl of a stand mixer and mix on medium speed for 2 to 3 minutes with a paddle attachment. Use a rubber spatula to scrape the sides of the bowl. Place the powdered sugar in the bowl with the creamed mixture, add the vanilla, and mix on low speed until the ingredients begin to come together. Increase the speed to medium and mix for 2 to 3 minutes, until fluffy. Proceed with the filling as directed.

Tips for Freezing: If you need to make the cakes ahead of time, first bake and cool them completely. Then put them in layers in a plastic container, placing wax paper or parchment between the layers. They will keep for 2 weeks in the freezer.

To defrost the cakes, uncover them and lay them flat in a single layer on baking sheets. Let them come to room temperature, about 3 to 4 hours, before filling. The filling should be made the day you plan to use it. Proceed with filling the cakes as directed.

Ingredients

Dark Mocha-Flavored Cakes

2 cups unbleached all-purpose flour

½ cup Dutch process cocoa

1¼ teaspoons baking soda

1 teaspoon salt

1 cup buttermilk

1 teaspoon pure vanilla extract

2 tablespoons instant coffee, reconstituted in 1 tablespoon warm water and cooled

¼ cup (½ stick) unsalted butter, at room temperature

¼ cup vegetable shortening

1 cup brown sugar, packed

1 large egg, lightly beaten

Kahlúa-Flavored Cakes

2 cups unbleached all-purpose flour

¾ teaspoon baking soda

¼ teaspoon salt

4 tablespoons (½ stick) unsalted butter, at room temperature

4 tablespoons vegetable shortening

¾ cup granulated sugar

3 large eggs, lightly beaten

1 tablespoon Kahlúa

⅓ cup sour cream, at room temperature

Kahlúa and Cream
Whoopie Pies

MAKES ABOUT 36 ASSEMBLED WHOOPIE PIES

These two-toned whoopie pies take a bit of time to make because of the double batch of cakes required. They are worth the extra effort because they contain all the rich flavors of the deliciously classic after-dinner drink that inspired them. The meringue powder can be found anywhere that sells cake decorating supplies.

1   Make the dark mocha-flavored cakes. Preheat the oven to 425°F and position an oven rack in the center. Lay 1 nonstick silicone baking mat or piece of parchment on each baking sheet.

2   In a medium mixing bowl, mix the flour, cocoa, baking soda, and salt together. Set aside.

3   Combine the buttermilk, vanilla, and reconstituted instant coffee in a small bowl. Set aside at room temperature.

4   Cream the butter with the shortening in the bowl of a stand mixer fitted with the paddle attachment on low speed until completely mixed and smooth, 1 to 2 minutes. Scrape the sides of the bowl well with a rubber spatula. Add the brown sugar and continue mixing on high speed for 3 minutes. Add the egg and mix until it is incorporated. Scrape the sides of the bowl again with the rubber spatula.

Filling

4 cups powdered sugar

3 tablespoons meringue powder

½ cup (1 stick) unsalted butter, at room temperature

3 tablespoons Kahlúa

1½ tablespoons milk

5   Turn the mixer on low speed and begin adding the flour and buttermilk in two alternating batches, beginning and ending with the flour mixture.

6   Scoop the batter into tablespoon-sized balls using a spring-loaded cookie scoop or a spoon and place about 2 inches apart on the prepared baking sheet. Bake for 8 to 10 minutes, until no indentation occurs when touched lightly with your finger. Remove from the baking sheet with a metal spatula and cool the cakes on a wire rack. Cool completely before filling.

7   Make the Kahlúa-flavored cakes. Preheat the oven to 425°F and position an oven rack in the center. Lay 1 nonstick silicone baking mat or piece of parchment on each baking sheet.

8   In a medium mixing bowl, mix the flour, baking soda, and salt together. Set aside.

9   Cream the butter with the shortening in the bowl of a stand mixer fitted with the paddle attachment on low speed until completely mixed and smooth, 1 to 2 minutes. Scrape the sides of the bowl well with a rubber spatula. Add the sugar and continue mixing on high for 3 minutes. Add the eggs and Kahlúa and mix until everything is incorporated. Scrape the sides of the bowl again with the rubber spatula.

10 Turn the mixer on low speed and begin adding the flour mixture and sour cream in two alternating batches, beginning and ending with the flour mixture.

11 Scoop the batter into tablespoon-sized balls using a spring-loaded cookie scoop or a spoon and place about 2 inches apart on the prepared baking sheet. Bake for 8 to 10 minutes, until

no indentation occurs when touched lightly with your finger. Remove from the baking sheet with a metal spatula and cool the cakes on a wire rack. Cool completely before filling.

12 Make the filling. Place the powdered sugar and meringue powder in the mixing bowl of a stand mixer fitted with the paddle attachment. Add the butter to the bowl and mix the ingredients together on low speed. The mixture will be very dry. With the motor still running on low speed, add the Kahlúa and milk. Turn the mixer off and scrape the sides of the bowl with a rubber spatula. Mix on medium-low speed for 1 more minute. Feel free to adjust the consistency with an additional tablespoon of milk if the filling seems too thick to spread easily over the cooled whoopie pies.

13 Assemble and fill the pies. Transfer the Kahlúa filling to a pastry bag fitted with a number 10 (or larger) pastry tip. Pipe the filling on the flat side of the mocha cakes. If you don't have a pastry bag, you can spread the filling with a knife or offset spatula. Match the Kahlúa cakes that are closest in size and place the second cake on top so that the filling is sandwiched between two flat sides. Store the assembled whoopie pies in a plastic container with a cookie rack fitted inside to prevent sticking. They are best eaten within 24 hours.

Optional: You can double the batch of either the mocha or Kahlúa whoopie cakes if you prefer a single-colored whoopie pie.

Alternate Baking Method: Use greased whoopie pie pans. Place 1½ tablespoons of batter into each cavity. Do not overfill the pans or your whoopie cakes will dome in the center.

Bake in a 350°F oven for 10 to 12 minutes, until no indentation occurs when touched lightly with your finger. Cool on a wire rack. Proceed with filling and assembling as directed.

Tips for Freezing: If you need to make the cakes ahead of time, first bake and cool them completely. Then put them in layers in a plastic container, placing wax paper or parchment between the layers. They will keep for 2 weeks in the freezer.

To defrost the cakes, uncover them and lay them flat in a single layer on baking sheets. Let them come to room temperature, about 3 to 4 hours, before filling. The filling should be made the day you plan to use it. Proceed with filling the cakes as directed.

German Chocolate
Whoopie Pies

MAKES ABOUT 24 ASSEMBLED PIES

If you thought you needed a fork to enjoy German chocolate cake, think again. Double chocolate cakes surround a cream filling infused with coconut, brown sugar, and toasted pecans.

1   Preheat the oven to 375°F and position an oven rack in the center. Lay 1 nonstick silicone baking mat or a piece of parchment on each baking sheet.

2   Make the cake. In a small heatproof bowl set over a double boiler on low heat, melt the chocolate chips. Stir with a heatproof rubber spatula until melted. Remove the bowl and set aside so that the chocolate can cool but not harden.

3   In a medium mixing bowl, mix the flour, baking soda, and salt together. Set aside.

4   Cream the butter with the brown sugar in the bowl of a stand mixer fitted with the paddle attachment on low speed until completely mixed. Increase the speed to medium for 1 to 2 minutes. Turn the mixer off and scrape the sides of the bowl well with a rubber spatula. Add the egg and vanilla, and mix until incorporated. Scrape the sides of the bowl well.

5   Add the cooled, melted chocolate, cocoa powder, and yogurt, and mix on low speed until all the ingredients come together.

....

Ingredients

Cake

⅓ cup (2 ounces) semisweet chocolate chips

2¼ cups unbleached all-purpose flour

¾ teaspoon baking soda

½ teaspoon salt

½ cup (1 stick) unsalted butter, at room temperature

¾ cup brown sugar, packed

1 egg, slightly beaten

½ teaspoon pure vanilla extract

2 tablespoons Dutch process cocoa powder

¼ cup plain yogurt, at room temperature

½ cup milk, at room temperature

Filling

½ cup pecans

4 tablespoons cream of coconut (such as Coco Lopez)

¼ cup brown sugar, packed

1¼ cups vegetable shortening

1½ cups marshmallow cream

1 cup powdered sugar

¼ cup unsweetened flaked coconut

¼ cup sweetened flaked coconut

¼ cup sweetened flaked coconut, toasted (reserved)

....

Turn the mixer off and scrape the sides of the bowl well.

6 Turn the mixer on low and begin adding the flour and the milk in 2 alternating batches, beginning with half of the flour and half of the milk. Repeat.

7 Scoop the batter into tablespoon-sized balls using a spring-loaded cookie scoop or a spoon and place about 2 inches apart on the prepared baking sheet. Bake the cakes one sheet at a time for 11 to 12 minutes, until the cakes are puffed. Transfer to a cooling rack and let cool completely.

8 Make the filling. Toast the pecans. Lower the oven temperature to 350°F. Spread the nuts in a single layer on a baking sheet. Bake for 6 to 8 minutes, until the nuts give off a strong, nutty aroma. Set aside to cool.

9 Meanwhile, in a small ramekin or bowl, combine the cream of coconut and brown sugar. Stir to distribute the liquid evenly. The brown sugar will begin to look melted. Set aside.

10 Place the shortening and marshmallow cream in the bowl of a stand mixer fitted with the paddle attachment. Cream them together on medium speed for 3 to 4 minutes. Use a rubber spatula to scrape the sides of the bowl. Place the powdered sugar in the bowl with the creamed mixture and mix for an additional 4 minutes on medium. Scrape the sides of the bowl well. Set aside briefly.

11 Transfer the cooled pecans to a food processor fitted with the blade attachment and chop until finely ground. You'll want to use the "pulse" button so you don't overgrind the nuts and end up with pecan butter. With the mixer turned off, transfer the nuts to the mixing bowl with the fluffy filling, and add the diluted brown sugar mixture and the two ¼ cups of flaked coconut (but not the toasted coconut). Turn the mixer on medium and mix for 2 to 3 minutes.

12 Assemble and fill the pies. Transfer the filling to a pastry bag fitted with a number 10 (or larger) pastry tip. Pipe the filling on the flat side of half of the cakes. If you don't have a pastry bag, you can spread the filling with a knife or offset spatula. Match cakes that are closest in size and place the second cake on top so that the filling is sandwiched between two flat sides. Place the toasted coconut on a plate or shallow dish and crumble slightly with your fingers. Roll the edges of the filled whoopie pies through the toasted coconut to coat the edges. Store the assembled whoopie pies in a plastic container with a cookie rack fitted inside to prevent sticking. They are best eaten within 24 hours.

Alternate Baking Method: Use greased whoopie pie pans. Place 1½ tablespoons of batter into each cavity. Do not overfill the pans or your whoopie cakes will dome in the center.

Bake in a 375°F oven for 10 to 12 minutes. Turn the cakes out onto a wire rack and cool completely before filling. Proceed with filling and assembling as directed.

Tips for Freezing: See page 74.

Ingredients

Cake

2 cups unbleached all-purpose flour

¾ teaspoon baking soda

¼ teaspoon salt

4 tablespoons (½ stick) unsalted butter, at room temperature

4 tablespoons vegetable shortening

¾ cup granulated sugar

3 large eggs, lightly beaten

2 teaspoons pure vanilla extract

⅓ cup sour cream, at room temperature

Filling

¾ cup Nutella

⅓ cup unsalted butter, at room temperature

½ cup powdered sugar

2 teaspoons unsweetened cocoa powder (optional)

. . . .

Classic Yellow Cake with Chocolate Cream

Whoopie Pies

MAKES ABOUT 20 ASSEMBLED PIES

Based on the classic yellow cake with chocolate frosting, the filling of these whoopie pies gets its unique flavor from the addition of Nutella.

1   Preheat the oven to 425°F and position an oven rack in the center. Lay 1 nonstick silicone baking mat or piece of parchment on each baking sheet.

2   Make the cake. In a medium mixing bowl, mix the flour, baking soda, and salt together. Set aside.

3   Place the butter and shortening in the bowl of a stand mixer fitted with the paddle attachment and cream on low speed until completely smooth. Scrape the sides of the bowl well with a rubber spatula. Add the sugar and continue mixing on high speed for 3 minutes. Add the eggs and vanilla and mix until everything is incorporated. Scrape the sides of the bowl again with the rubber spatula.

4   Turn the mixer on low speed and begin adding the flour mixture and sour cream in two alternating batches, beginning and ending with the flour mixture.

5 Scoop the batter into tablespoon-sized balls using a spring-loaded cookie scoop or a spoon and place about 2 inches apart on the prepared baking sheet. Bake 8 to 10 minutes, until no indentation appears when touched lightly with your finger. Remove from the baking sheet with a metal spatula and cool the cakes on a wire rack. Cool completely before filling.

6 Make the filling. Mix the Nutella and butter in the bowl of a stand mixer fitted with the paddle attachment on low speed. Scrape the sides of the bowl and add the powdered sugar. Mix until smooth on low speed. If you prefer more chocolate flavor, add 2 teaspoons of cocoa powder and mix well.

7 Assemble and fill the pies. Transfer the chocolate filling to a pastry bag fitted with a number 10 (or larger) pastry tip. Pipe the filling on the flat side of half the cakes. If you don't have a pastry bag, you can spread the filling with a knife or offset spatula. Match the cakes that are closest in size and place the second cake on top so that the filling is sandwiched between two flat sides. Store the assembled whoopie pies in a plastic container with a cookie rack fitted inside to prevent sticking. They are best eaten within 24 hours.

Alternate Baking Method: Use greased whoopie pie pans. Place 1½ tablespoons of batter into each cavity. Do not overfill the pans or your whoopie cakes will dome in the center.

Bake in a 350°F oven for 10 to 12 minutes, until no indentation appears when touched lightly with your finger. Cool on a wire rack. Proceed with filling and assembling as directed.

Tips for Freezing: If you need to make the cakes ahead of time, first bake and cool them completely. Then put them in layers in a plastic container, placing wax paper or parchment between the layers. They will keep for 2 weeks in the freezer.

To defrost the cakes, uncover them and lay them flat in a single layer on baking sheets. Let them come to room temperature, about 3 to 4 hours, before filling. The filling should be made the day you plan to use it. Proceed with filling the cakes as directed.

Red Velvet
Whoopie Pies

MAKES ABOUT 20 ASSEMBLED PIES

Here's a simple recipe that's easy enough for young bakers to follow with a little adult supervision. But don't be surprised that you'll both love eating these whoopie pies as much as baking them. We've used red powdered food coloring in this recipe, which can be easily found at craft, cake, and candy supply stores. Two brands to look for are CK Country Kitchen and Candy-n-Cake.

1   Preheat the oven to 375°F and position an oven rack in the center. Lay 1 nonstick silicone baking mat or a piece of parchment on each baking sheet.

2   Make the cake. In a medium mixing bowl, mix the flour and cocoa powder together. Set aside.

3   Place the shortening in the bowl of a stand mixer fitted with the paddle attachment and cream on low speed until completely smooth. Scrape the sides of the bowl well with a rubber spatula. Add the sugars and continue mixing on high speed for 3 minutes. Add the eggs and mix until everything is incorporated, about 3 minutes. Scrape the sides of the bowl again with the rubber spatula.

4   In a small dish or ramekin, stir the vanilla into the red powdered food coloring. Set aside.

Ingredients

Cake

2½ cups self-rising flour

2 tablespoons cocoa powder

½ cup vegetable shortening

1 cup granulated sugar

½ cup brown sugar, packed

2 eggs, lightly beaten

2 teaspoons pure vanilla extract

2 tablespoons red powdered food coloring (found at cake and candy supply stores)

1 cup buttermilk

Filling

½ cup (1 stick) unsalted butter

3 cups powdered sugar

½ cup (4 ounces) heavy cream

½ teaspoon vanilla extract

Pinch of salt (optional)

5   Turn the mixer on low and add half of the flour mixture and half of the buttermilk. Repeat with the remaining portions. Mix only until incorporated. Scrape the sides of the bowl well with a rubber spatula.

6   Add the food coloring and vanilla mixture with the mixer speed on the lowest setting. When most of the color is beginning to blend into the batter, turn the mixer off and continue mixing by hand only until the color is evenly distributed.

7   Scoop the batter into tablespoon-sized balls using a spring-loaded cookie scoop or a spoon and place about 2 inches apart on the prepared baking sheet. Bake 11 to 13 minutes, until no indentation appears when touched lightly with your finger. Remove from the baking sheet with a metal spatula and cool the cakes on a wire rack. Cool completely before filling.

8   Make the filling. Whip the butter in the bowl of a stand mixer fitted with the paddle attachment on low speed. Scrape the sides of the bowl and add the powdered sugar, cream, and vanilla. Mix on low speed until the sugar begins to incorporate into the other ingredients. Turn the mixer to medium for 1 to 2 minutes, until the buttercream is fluffy and easily spreadable. You may choose to add a very small pinch of salt to your buttercream if you want to offset some of the sweetness.

9   Assemble and fill the pies. Transfer the filling to a pastry bag fitted with a number 10 (or larger) pastry tip. Pipe the filling on the flat side of half of the cakes. If you don't have a pastry bag, you can spread the filling with a knife or offset spatula. Match the cakes that are closest in size and place the second cake on top so that the filling is sandwiched between two flat sides. Store the assembled whoopie pies in a plastic container with a cookie rack fitted inside to prevent sticking. They are best eaten within 24 hours.

Alternate Baking Method: Use greased whoopie pie pans, prior to filling. Place 1½ tablespoons of batter into each cavity. Do not overfill the pans or your whoopie cakes will dome in the center.

Bake in a 350°F oven for 11 to 13 minutes, until no indentation appears when touched lightly with a finger. Cool on a wire rack. Proceed with filling and assembling as directed.

Tips for Freezing: If you need to make the cakes ahead of time, first bake and cool them completely. Then put them in layers in a plastic container, placing wax paper or parchment between the layers. They will keep for 2 weeks in the freezer.

To defrost the cakes, uncover them and lay them flat in a single layer on baking sheets. Let them come to room temperature, about 3 to 4 hours, before filling. The filling should be made the day you plan to use it. Proceed with filling the cakes as directed.

Chocolate Whoopie Pies
with Salted Caramel Filling

MAKES ABOUT 20 ASSEMBLED PIES

In this recipe sweet caramel is balanced with just the right amount of salt to add sophistication to a childhood treat that's hard for any adult to resist. The peppermint filing variation is a holiday treat that's certain to become a classic.

1   Preheat the oven to 425°F and position an oven rack in the center. Lay 1 nonstick silicone baking mat or a piece of parchment on each baking sheet.

2   Make the cake. In a medium mixing bowl, mix the flour, cocoa, baking soda, and salt together. Set aside.

3   Combine the buttermilk and vanilla in a small bowl. Set aside at room temperature.

4   Cream the butter with the shortening in the bowl of a stand mixer fitted with the paddle attachment on low speed until completely mixed. Scrape the sides of the bowl well with the rubber spatula. Add the brown sugar and continue mixing on high speed for 3 minutes until the mixture is light brown and fluffy. Add the egg and mix until incorporated. Scrape the sides of the bowl again.

Ingredients

Cake

2 cups unbleached all-purpose flour

½ cup Dutch process cocoa

1¼ teaspoons baking soda

1 teaspoon salt

1 cup buttermilk

1 teaspoon pure vanilla extract

¼ cup (½ stick) unsalted butter, at room temperature

¼ cup vegetable shortening

1 cup brown sugar, packed

1 large egg, lightly beaten

Filling

4 ounces caramel candies (12 to 15 candies), wrappers removed

1 tablespoon heavy cream

1 tablespoon plus 1 teaspoon kosher salt

¾ cup vegetable shortening

1 cup powdered sugar

1 teaspoon caramel-flavored syrup

5 Turn the mixer on low and begin adding the flour mixture and buttermilk in two alternating batches, beginning and ending with the flour mixture.

6 Scoop the batter into tablespoon-sized balls using a spring-loaded cookie scoop or a spoon and place about 2 inches apart on the prepared baking sheet. Bake the cakes one sheet at a time for 8 minutes, until the cakes are puffed. Transfer to a cooling rack and let cool completely.

7 Make the filling. Place the caramels in a small heatproof bowl. Set the bowl just above a hot water bath, using a small saucepan containing boiling water. Lower the heat so the water comes to a gentle simmer. Stir with a heatproof rubber spatula until the caramels are soft and completely melted. Remove the water bath and bowl from the heat.

8 Measure the cream in a microwave-safe measuring cup. Place in the microwave for about 12 seconds to remove any trace of cold.

9 Remove the bowl of melted caramels from the water bath and place the bowl on a heat-resistant work surface. Add 1 teaspoon kosher salt and the warm cream to the melted caramel. Stir continuously until the salt, cream, and caramels are completely combined. Cool for 5 minutes.

10 Pour the cooled caramel mixture into a medium mixing bowl and add the shortening. In a stand mixer, cream together using the paddle attachment. When completely combined, add 1 cup powdered sugar and mix well. Add the remaining 1 tablespoon kosher salt and the caramel-flavored syrup. Mix completely.

11 Assemble and fill the pies. Transfer the caramel filling to a pastry bag fitted with a number 10 (or larger) pastry tip. Pipe the filling on the flat side of half of the cakes. If you don't have a pastry bag, you can spread the filling with a knife or offset spatula. Match cakes that are closest in size and place the second cake on top so that the filling is sandwiched between two flat sides. Store the assembled whoopie pies in a plastic container with a cookie rack fitted inside to prevent sticking. They are best eaten within 24 hours.

Alternate Baking Method: Use greased whoopie pie pans. Place 1½ tablespoons of batter into each cavity. Do not overfill the pans or your whoopie cakes will dome in the center.

Bake in a 350°F oven for 10 to 12 minutes, until no indentation occurs when touched lightly with your finger. Cool on a wire rack. Proceed with filling and assembling as directed.

Tips for Freezing: See page 74.

Peppermint Whoopie Pies

Make and bake the cakes as directed, but fill the centers with peppermint filling and roll in crushed peppermint candy.

●●●●●●●●●●●●●●●●●●●●●●●●●●●●●●●●●●●●●

Peppermint Filling

¼ cup (½ stick) unsalted butter, at room temperature

⅓ cup vegetable shortening

1 cup marshmallow cream

½ cup powdered sugar

1 tablespoon peppermint schnapps

½ cup crushed peppermint candies

●●●●●●●●●●●●●●●●●●●●●●●●●●●●●●●●●●●●●

1   Place the butter and vegetable shortening in a medium mixing bowl of a stand mixer, and beat on low speed with a paddle attachment. Add the marshmallow cream and increase the speed to medium. Beat for 3 minutes.

2   Add the powdered sugar and continue beating on medium speed for an additional 3 minutes.

3   Add the peppermint schnapps, beating on low speed for 1 minute. Pipe the filling between two cakes as directed.

4   Place the crushed peppermint candies on a plate or other shallow container such as a pie tin. After assembling the whoopie pies, gently roll the edges along the crushed peppermint to coat. Store as directed.

Ingredients

Cake

3 cups unbleached all-purpose flour

1½ teaspoons baking powder

½ teaspoon salt

¾ cup (about 7 whole crackers) finely ground graham cracker crumbs

½ cup (1 stick) unsalted butter, at room temperature

¾ cup granulated sugar

¾ cup brown sugar

1 egg

2 teaspoons pure vanilla extract

1 cup buttermilk, at room temperature

2 tablespoons honey

Filling

2 cups powdered sugar

4 tablespoons (½ stick) unsalted butter, at room temperature

Pinch of salt

3 tablespoons heavy cream

2½ tablespoons Key lime juice (such as Nellie and Joe's or from 5 fresh Key limes)

Zest of 1 lime (optional)

Key Lime
Whoopie Pies

MAKES ABOUT 20 ASSEMBLED PIES

The secret ingredient in this recipe is crushed graham crackers folded into the cake batter. If you want a true Key lime flavor be sure to purchase Key limes or Key lime juice. The subtle tartness of Key lime plays wonderfully off the delicate sweetness of the graham cakes. This recipe is best eaten the day it is made.

1   Preheat the oven to 375°F and position an oven rack in the center. Lay 1 nonstick silicone baking mat or piece of parchment on each baking sheet.

2   Make the cake. In a medium mixing bowl, mix the flour, baking powder, and salt. Blend with a fork to evenly distribute the dry ingredients.

3   In the bowl of a food processor fitted with the blade attachment, place about 7 whole broken graham crackers. Pulse on and off until all the crackers have come to a fine crumb stage and no chunks exist.

4   Cream the butter with both sugars in the bowl of a stand mixer fitted with the paddle attachment on medium speed until completely mixed, about 3 minutes. Scrape the sides of the bowl well with a rubber spatula. Add the egg and vanilla and mix on medium speed for 2 to 3 minutes, until the mixture is smooth. Scrape the sides of the bowl well with the rubber spatula.

5 Turn the mixer on low and begin adding the flour and the buttermilk in two alternating batches beginning with half the flour and half the buttermilk. Using a rubber spatula, scrape the sides of the bowl well.

6 Add the honey and graham cracker crumbs. Mix only until the ingredients are incorporated.

7 Scoop the batter into tablespoon-sized portions using a spring-loaded cookie scoop or a spoon and place about 2 inches apart on the prepared baking sheet. Bake the cakes one sheet at a time for 11 to 13 minutes, until your finger does not leave an indentation in the cakes when touched lightly. Transfer to a cooling rack and let cool completely.

8 Make the filling. Place the powdered sugar and butter in the medium bowl of a stand mixer and mix on low speed for 2 to 3 minutes with a paddle attachment. The mixture will look very dry. Use a rubber spatula to scrape the sides of the bowl. Add the salt, heavy cream, Key lime juice, and zest, if using. Mix on low speed until the ingredients begin to come together. Increase the speed to medium and mix for 2 to 3 minutes, until fluffy.

9 Assemble and fill the pies. Transfer the brown sugar filling into a pastry bag fitted with a number 10 (or larger) pastry tip. Pipe the filling on the flat side of half the cakes. If you don't have a pastry bag, you can spread the filling with a knife or offset spatula. Match cakes that are closest in size and place the second cake on top so that the filling is sandwiched between two flat sides. Store the assembled whoopie pies in a plastic container with a cookie rack fitted inside to prevent sticking. However, they are best eaten within 24 hours.

Alternate Baking Method: Use greased whoopie pie pans. Place 1½ tablespoons of batter into each cavity. Do not overfill the pans or your whoopie cakes will dome in the center.

Bake in a 350°F oven for 11 to 13 minutes. Turn the cakes out onto a wire rack and cool completely before filling. Proceed with filling and assembling as directed.

Tips for Freezing: Unlike the other whoopie pie recipes in this book, these particular whoopie pies don't freeze well and should be enjoyed the day they are made.

Black Forest
Whoopie Pies

MAKES ABOUT 20 ASSEMBLED PIES

These are a hand-sized twist on the classic Black Forest cake. Tart cherry marshmallow filling is sandwiched between chocolate cakes infused with cherry liqueur.

1   Preheat the oven to 425°F and position an oven rack in the center. Lay 1 nonstick silicone baking mat or piece of parchment on each baking sheet.

2   Make the cake. In a medium mixing bowl, mix the flour, cocoa, baking soda, and salt together. Set aside.

3   Combine the buttermilk, vanilla, and cherry liqueur in a small bowl. Set aside at room temperature.

4   Cream the butter with the shortening in the bowl of a stand mixer fitted with the paddle attachment on low speed until completely mixed and smooth. Scrape the sides of the bowl well with a rubber spatula. Add the brown sugar and continue mixing on high for 3 minutes. Add the egg and mix until incorporated. Scrape the sides of the bowl again with the rubber spatula.

5   Turn the mixer on low speed and begin adding the flour mixture and the buttermilk mixture in two alternating batches, beginning and ending with the flour mixture.

Ingredients

Cake

2 cups unbleached all-purpose flour

½ cup Dutch process cocoa

1¼ teaspoons baking soda

1 teaspoon salt

1 cup buttermilk

1 teaspoon pure vanilla extract

1 tablespoon cherry liqueur

¼ cup (½ stick) unsalted butter, at room temperature

¼ cup vegetable shortening

1 cup brown sugar, packed

1 large egg, lightly beaten

Filling

½ cup dried cherries

2 tablespoons cherry liqueur

¼ cup (½ stick) unsalted butter, at room temperature

¼ cup vegetable shortening

1 cup marshmallow cream

1 cup powdered sugar

Chocolate sprinkles (optional)

6 Scoop the batter into tablespoon-sized balls using a spring-loaded cookie scoop or a spoon and place about 2 inches apart on the prepared baking sheet. Bake for 8 to 10 minutes, until no indentation occurs when lightly touched with your finger. Remove from the baking sheet with a metal spatula and cool the cakes on a wire rack. Cool completely before filling.

7 Make the filling. Place the dried cherries in a small microwave-safe ramekin or dish. Add the cherry liqueur. Cover the dish with plastic wrap or other microwave-safe covering and microwave on high for about 15 seconds to create steam and reconstitute the cherries. Keep the dish covered and set it aside to cool. When the cherries have cooled, spoon them onto a cutting board, reserving the liquid in the dish. Use a chef's knife to chop the cherries into very small pieces. Return the chopped cherries to the cherry liqueur and reserve.

8 Place the butter and vegetable shortening in the bowl of a stand mixer fitted with the paddle attachment. Beat on low speed for 1 to 2 minutes. Add the marshmallow cream and increase the speed to medium. Beat for 3 minutes. Add the powdered sugar and continue beating on medium speed for an additional 3 minutes. Scrape the sides of the bowl well with a rubber spatula. Add

the chopped reconstituted cherries and the remaining cherry liqueur to the filling mixture and mix until it is fully incorporated.

9 Assemble and fill the pies. Transfer the cherry filling to a pastry bag fitted with a number 10 (or larger) pastry tip. Pipe the filling on the flat side of half the cakes. If you don't have a pastry bag, you can spread the filling with a knife or offset spatula. Match cakes that are closest in size and place the second cake on top so that the filling is sandwiched between two flat sides. Store the assembled whoopie pies in a plastic container with a cookie rack fitted inside to prevent sticking. They are best eaten within 24 hours.

10 If you like, pour chocolate sprinkles in the bottom of a shallow bowl or pie plate. Gently roll the edges of the whoopie pies in the chocolate sprinkles to decorate the edges.

Alternate Baking Method: Use greased whoopie pie pans. Place 1½ tablespoons of batter into each cavity. Do not overfill the pans or your whoopie pies will dome in the center.

Bake in a 350°F oven for 8 to 10 minutes, until no indentation occurs when lightly touched with your finger. Cool on a wire rack. Proceed with filling and assembling as directed.

Tips for Freezing: See page 74.

Ingredients

Cake

4 cups unbleached all-purpose flour

3 teaspoons cinnamon

1 teaspoon salt

1 teaspoon baking soda

¼ teaspoon finely ground black pepper

¼ teaspoon ginger

2 teaspoons unsweetened cocoa powder

6 tablespoons (¾ stick) unsalted butter, at room temperature

¼ cup vegetable shortening

¾ cup brown sugar, packed

1 large egg, lightly beaten

¾ cup light molasses

1 cup buttermilk, at room temperature

Filling

½ cup (1 stick) unsalted butter, at room temperature

½ cup vegetable shortening

4 cups powdered sugar

3 tablespoons milk

½ teaspoon orange oil

Pinch of salt

1 teaspoon grated orange zest (optional)

Gingerbread Whoopie Pies
with Orange Buttercream Filling

MAKES ABOUT 24 ASSEMBLED PIES

In this recipe the gingerbread cakes have a hint of crushed black pepper, but it's softened by the sweetness of the orange buttercream.

1 Preheat the oven to 375°F and position an oven rack in the center. Lay 1 nonstick silicone baking mat or piece of parchment on each baking sheet.

2 Make the cake. In a medium mixing bowl, mix the flour, cinnamon, salt, baking soda, black pepper, ginger, and cocoa powder together. Set aside.

3 Cream the butter with the shortening in the bowl of a stand mixer fitted with the paddle attachment on low speed until completely mixed. Scrape the sides of the bowl well with a rubber spatula. Add the brown sugar and continue mixing on high speed for 3 minutes, until the mixture is light brown and fluffy. Add the egg and mix until incorporated. Scrape the sides of the bowl again and add the molasses. Mix on low speed until completely mixed together. Scrape the sides of the bowl well.

4   Turn the mixer on low speed and add the flour mixture and the buttermilk in two alternating batches, beginning and ending with the flour mixture.

5   Scoop the batter into tablespoon-sized balls using a spring-loaded cookie scoop or a spoon and place about 2 inches apart on the baking sheet. Bake the cakes one sheet at a time for 10 to 12 minutes, until the cakes are puffed. Transfer to a cooling rack and let cool completely.

6   Make the filling. Place the butter and shortening in the bowl of a stand mixer fitted with the paddle attachment. Cream them together on medium speed for 1 to 2 minutes. Use a rubber spatula to scrape the sides of the bowl. Place the powdered sugar in the bowl with the creamed mixture, and add the milk, orange oil, and salt.

Add the orange zest, if using. Turn the mixer on low speed until the ingredients begin to come together. Increase the speed to medium and mix for 1 to 2 minutes, or until easily spreadable.

7   Assemble and fill the pies. Transfer the orange buttercream to a pastry bag fitted with a number 10 (or larger) pastry tip. Pipe the filling on the flat side of half the cakes. If you don't have a pastry bag, you can spread the filling with a knife or offset spatula. Match cakes that are closest in size and place the second cake on top so the filling is sandwiched between two flat sides. Store the assembled whoopie pies in a plastic container with a cookie rack fitted inside to prevent sticking. They are best eaten within 24 hours.

Alternate Baking Method: Use greased whoopie pie pans. Place 1½ tablespoons of batter into each cavity. Do not overfill the pans or your whoopie cakes will dome in the center.

Bake in a 375°F oven for 10 to 12 minutes. Turn the cakes out onto a wire rack and cool completely before filling. Proceed with filling and assembling as directed.

Tips for Freezing: If you need to make the cakes ahead of time, first bake and cool them completely. Then put them in layers in a plastic container, placing wax paper or parchment between the layers. They will keep for 2 weeks in the freezer.

To defrost the cakes, uncover them and lay them flat in a single layer on baking sheets. Let them come to room temperature, about 3 to 4 hours, before filling. The filling should be made the day you plan to use it. Proceed with filling the cakes as directed.

Doughnuts

Blueberry Buttermilk
Doughnuts

MAKES 16 LARGE OR 64 MINI DOUGHNUTS

Blueberries may seem unusual in a doughnut, but paired with this refreshing orange glaze you will find it's the perfect combination of tart and sweet! These are a healthier doughnut because they are baked instead of fried, but you will need either a standard-size doughnut pan or a standard-size mini doughnut pan for baking these.

1   Preheat the oven to 375°F and position an oven rack in the center. Lightly coat the doughnut pans with nonstick cooking spray.

2   Make the doughnuts. In a large bowl, combine the flour, granulated sugar, baking powder, baking soda, cinnamon, and orange zest with a whisk. Melt the butter in a small pot over low heat and set aside. In a medium bowl, combine the melted butter, buttermilk, eggs, and vanilla with a whisk until foamy, 1 to 2 minutes. Pour the egg mixture into the flour mixture and stir with a large wooden spoon until completely combined. Gently fold in the blueberries until just combined. Do not overmix. Using a pastry bag fitted with a 1-inch round tip, divide the batter equally (using even pressure) between the pans, filling about halfway full. Alternatively, you can use a gallon-sized resealable plastic storage bag. Fill the bag and using scissors, remove 1 inch from one of the bottom corners and proceed with filling the pans as described above.

Ingredients

Doughnuts

3 cups unbleached all-purpose flour

1 cup granulated sugar

2 teaspoons baking powder

1 teaspoon baking soda

1 teaspoon cinnamon

1 tablespoon grated orange zest

½ cup (1 stick) salted butter

1 cup buttermilk

3 large eggs, beaten

2 teaspoons pure vanilla extract

1 cup fresh or frozen blueberries

Glaze

1½ cups powdered sugar, sifted

3 tablespoons fresh orange juice

2 teaspoons grated orange zest

3 Bake for 8 to 10 minutes, until the doughnuts spring back when lightly touched. Remove from the oven, invert the doughnuts onto a rack, and allow to cool completely.

4 Make the glaze. In a medium bowl, combine the powdered sugar, orange juice, and orange zest with a whisk, mixing until smooth.

5 Glaze the doughnuts. Dip the top of each doughnut into the glaze and lift, allowing the excess to drip back into the bowl. Place the doughnuts on a platter and serve. These doughnuts are best served fresh.

Sticky
Toffee Doughnuts

MAKES 10 LARGE OR 40 MINI DOUGHNUTS

This may be the first doughnut you will eat with a fork, but it's well worth the effort. Chopped dates and cinnamon complement the doughnut and the buttery brown sugar glaze finishes it off perfectly. These are a healthier doughnut because they are baked instead of fried, but you will need either a standard-size doughnut pan or a standard-size mini doughnut pan for baking these.

1   Preheat the oven to 350°F and position an oven rack in the center. Lightly coat the doughnut pans with nonstick cooking spray.

2   Make the doughnuts. Put the chopped dates and water in a small saucepan and bring to a boil over high heat, then immediately remove from the heat and set aside. This will allow the dates to absorb moisture and plump up. Put the butter and granulated sugar in the bowl of a stand mixer fitted with the paddle attachment and cream on medium speed for 2 to 3 minutes, until light and fluffy. Scrape the sides of the bowl with a rubber spatula as needed. With the machine running on low speed, add the egg and vanilla and mix until incorporated.

3   In a medium bowl, combine the flour, baking powder, baking soda, salt, and cinnamon with a whisk. With the machine running on low speed, add half the dry ingredients and mix

Ingredients

Doughnuts

1 cup chopped dates

¼ cup water

6 tablespoons (¾ stick) salted butter, at room temperature

¼ cup granulated sugar

1 large egg

1 teaspoon pure vanilla extract

1½ cups unbleached all-purpose flour

1 teaspoon baking powder

¼ teaspoon baking soda

¼ teaspoon salt

1 teaspoon cinnamon

½ cup buttermilk

Glaze

1 cup heavy cream

½ cup brown sugar

2 tablespoons (¼ stick) salted butter

until just combined, add the buttermilk and mix in, then add the rest of the dry ingredients and mix until just combined. Transfer the cooled dates to a fine-mesh strainer and remove any remaining liquid by pressing with the back of a wooden spoon. Gently fold the dates into the batter with a rubber spatula. Using a pastry bag fitted with a ½-inch round tip, divide the batter equally (using even pressure) between the pans, filling approximately halfway full. Alternatively, you can use a gallon-sized resealable plastic storage bag. Fill the bag and using scissors, remove ½ inch from one of the bottom corners and proceed filling the pans as described.

4   Bake for 8 to 10 minutes, until the doughnuts spring back when lightly touched. Remove from the oven, invert the doughnuts onto a rack, and allow to cool.

5   Make the glaze. Put the cream and brown sugar in a medium saucepan and whisk until combined. Bring to a boil over high heat, turn the heat to medium, and allow to boil for approximately 10 minutes, or until reduced by one third. Do not stir, as the mixture will sputter. Remove from the heat and allow to rest for 10 minutes. Whisk in the butter until completely combined. Pour the glaze into a medium bowl.

6   Glaze the doughnuts. Place one doughnut in the glaze and turn, using a large slotted spoon to evenly coat the doughnut. Remove, using the spoon, and place back on the rack. Repeat until all the doughnuts are coated with the glaze. Because of the sticky glaze, these doughnuts are best eaten with a fork.

Old-Fashioned
Spice Doughnuts

MAKES 9 LARGE OR 36 MINI DOUGHNUTS

The warm aroma of cinnamon and allspice will remind you of Grandma's kitchen. The buttery glaze flecked with fresh vanilla seeds is a lovely complement to this classic doughnut. These are a healthier doughnut because they are baked instead of fried, but you will need either a standard-size doughnut pan or a standard-size mini doughnut pan for baking these.

1   Preheat the oven to 350°F and position an oven rack in the center. Lightly coat the doughnut pans with nonstick cooking spray.

2   Make the doughnuts. Put the butter, granulated sugar, and brown sugar in the bowl of a stand mixer fitted with the paddle attachment and cream on medium speed for 2 to 3 minutes, until light and fluffy. Scrape the sides of the bowl with a rubber spatula as needed. With the machine running on low speed, add the egg and vanilla and mix until incorporated.

3   In a medium bowl, combine the flour, baking powder, baking soda, salt, cinnamon, and allspice with a whisk. With the machine running on low speed, add half the dry ingredients and mix until just combined. Add the buttermilk and mix in, then add the rest of the dry ingredients and mix until just combined. Using a pastry bag fitted with a ½-inch

Doughnuts

6 tablespoons (¾ stick) salted butter, at room temperature

¼ cup granulated sugar

¼ cup brown sugar, firmly packed

1 large egg

1 teaspoon pure vanilla extract

1½ cups unbleached all-purpose flour

1 teaspoon baking powder

¼ teaspoon baking soda

¼ teaspoon salt

1 teaspoon cinnamon

½ teaspoon allspice

½ cup buttermilk

Glaze

1½ cups powdered sugar

2 tablespoons (¼ stick) salted butter, melted

6 tablespoons whole milk

½ vanilla bean

round tip, divide the batter equally (using even pressure) between the pans, filling approximately halfway full. Alternatively, you can use a gallon-sized resealable plastic storage bag. Fill the bag and using scissors, remove ½ inch from one of the bottom corners and proceed filling the pans as described.

4   Bake for 8 to 10 minutes, until the doughnuts spring back when lightly touched. Remove from the oven, invert the doughnuts onto a rack, and allow to cool completely.

5   Make the glaze. In a medium bowl, combine the powdered sugar, melted butter, and milk with a whisk, mixing until smooth; set aside. Place the vanilla bean on a cutting board and split it in half lengthwise with a small paring knife. Using the dull side of the knife, gently scrape out the vanilla seeds from each half and add them to the glaze mixture, whisking until completely incorporated.

6   Glaze the doughnuts. Dip the top of each doughnut into the glaze and lift, allowing the excess to drip back into the bowl. Whisk the glaze from time to time to prevent a crust from forming. Place the doughnuts on a platter and serve. These doughnuts are best served fresh.

Peanut Butter
Doughnuts

MAKES 12 LARGE OR 48 MINI DOUGHNUTS

A chocolate glaze enhances the subtle peanut flavor of the doughnuts and the chopped peanuts provide a welcome crunch. These are a healthier doughnut because they are baked instead of fried, but you will need either a standard-size doughnut pan or a standard-size mini doughnut pan for baking these.

1   Preheat the oven to 350°F and position an oven rack in the center. Lightly coat the doughnut pans with nonstick cooking spray.

2   Make the doughnuts. Put the butter and the two sugars in the bowl of a stand mixer fitted with the paddle attachment and cream on medium speed for 2 to 3 minutes, until light and fluffy. Add the peanut butter and mix on low speed to combine. Scrape the sides of the bowl with a rubber spatula as needed. With the mixer running on low speed, add the eggs one at a time, allowing each one to be incorporated before adding the next. Add the vanilla and mix to combine.

3   In a medium bowl, combine the flour, baking powder, and baking soda with a whisk. With the machine running on low speed, add half the flour mixture and mix until just combined. Add the sour cream, mix until incorporated, and add the rest of the flour mixture, mixing until just combined. Using a pastry

Ingredients

Doughnuts

½ cup (1 stick) salted butter, at room temperature

1 cup brown sugar, firmly packed

½ cup granulated sugar

¼ cup creamy peanut butter

3 large eggs

1 teaspoon pure vanilla extract

1½ cups unbleached all-purpose flour

¼ teaspoon baking powder

⅛ teaspoon baking soda

¼ cup sour cream

Glaze

½ cup semisweet chocolate morsels

6 tablespoons (¾ stick) salted butter

½ cup dry roasted peanuts, chopped

bag fitted with a ½-inch round tip, divide the batter equally (using even pressure) between the pans, filling about halfway full. Alternatively, you can use a gallon-sized resealable plastic storage bag. Fill the bag and using scissors, remove ½ inch from one of the bottom corners and proceed filling the pans as described.

4   Bake for 12 to 14 minutes, until the doughnuts spring back when lightly touched. Remove from the oven, invert the doughnuts onto a rack, and allow to cool completely.

5   Make the glaze. Place the chocolate morsels in a medium heatproof bowl and place over a small pot of simmering water, being sure

the bowl is not touching the water. Turn off the burner and allow the chocolate to melt completely, occasionally stirring with a heatproof rubber spatula. Stir in the butter until completely melted and combined. Remove the bowl from the pot and set aside.

6   Glaze the doughnuts. Dip the top of each doughnut into the glaze and lift, allowing the excess to drip back into the bowl. While the glaze is wet, evenly distribute the peanuts on top of the doughnuts. The glaze will harden slightly as it cools. Place the doughnuts on a platter and serve. These doughnuts are best served fresh.

Ingredients

Doughnuts

6 tablespoons (¾ stick) salted
    butter, at room temperature

½ cup sugar

1 large egg

½ teaspoon pure vanilla extract

1½ cups unbleached all-purpose
    flour

1 teaspoon baking powder

¼ teaspoon salt

¼ teaspoon nutmeg

½ cup buttermilk

Coating

6 tablespoons (¾ stick) salted
    butter, melted

¾ cup sugar

1 teaspoon cinnamon

. . . .

nutmeg
Puff Doughnuts

MAKES 9 LARGE OR 36 MINI DOUGHNUTS

**Dipping these doughnuts in melted butter before tossing in cinnamon
sugar ensures a soft texture that is enhanced by the spicy warmth of
the nutmeg. Nutmeg can be purchased ground or whole. Try grinding
your own using a small grater and you will surely notice the difference.
These are a healthier doughnut because they are baked instead of fried,
but you will need either a standard-size doughnut pan or a standard-
size mini doughnut pan for baking these.**

1   Preheat the oven to 350°F and position an oven rack in the
    center. Lightly coat the doughnut pans with nonstick cooking
    spray.

2   Make the doughnuts. Put the butter and sugar in the bowl of
    a stand mixer fitted with the paddle attachment and cream on
    medium speed for 2 to 3 minutes, until light and fluffy. Scrape
    the sides of the bowl with a rubber spatula as needed. With
    the machine running on low speed, add the egg and mix until
    incorporated. Add the vanilla and mix to combine.

3   In a medium bowl, combine the flour, baking powder, salt, and
    nutmeg and combine with a whisk. With the machine running
    on low speed, add half the dry ingredients and mix until just
    combined. Add the buttermilk and mix in, then add the rest of
    the dry ingredients and mix until just combined. Using a pastry
    bag fitted with a ½-inch round tip, divide the batter equally

(using even pressure) between the pans, filling approximately halfway full. Alternatively, you can use a gallon-sized resealable plastic storage bag. Fill the bag and using scissors, remove ½ inch from one of the bottom corners and proceed filling the pans as described.

4   Bake for 10 to 12 minutes, until the doughnuts spring back when lightly touched. Remove from the oven, invert the doughnuts onto a rack, and allow to cool for 5 minutes.

5   Make the coating. Place the melted butter in a medium bowl and set aside. In another medium bowl, combine the sugar and cinnamon with a whisk.

6   Coat the doughnuts. Quickly dip the slightly warm doughnuts in the melted butter, being sure to coat both sides, then toss in the sugar mixture. Place on a rack and allow to cool completely. Serve immediately or store in an airtight container at room temperature for up to 1 day.

Ingredients

Doughnuts

1 cup unbleached all-purpose flour

½ cup granulated sugar

1 teaspoon baking powder

¼ teaspoon salt

2 large eggs, beaten

3 tablespoons vegetable oil

2 tablespoons buttermilk

1 teaspoon pure vanilla extract

Glaze

¾ cup powdered sugar, sifted

1 tablespoon water

1 cup sweetened flaked coconut

Snowball
Doughnuts

MAKES 6 LARGE OR 24 MINI DOUGHNUTS

Sweet flaky coconut adds a delightful flavor to this doughnut. You might want to tint the coconut with a drop or two of pink food coloring to bring back memories of those childhood treats. These are a healthier doughnut because they are baked instead of fried, but you will need either a standard-size doughnut pan or a standard-size mini doughnut pan for baking these.

1   Preheat the oven to 375°F and position an oven rack in the center. Lightly coat the doughnut pans with nonstick cooking spray.

2   Make the doughnuts. In a large bowl, combine the flour, granulated sugar, baking powder, and salt with a whisk. In a medium bowl, combine the eggs, oil, buttermilk, and vanilla with a whisk until foamy, 1 to 2 minutes. Pour the egg mixture into the flour mixture and stir, using a large wooden spoon, until completely combined. Using a pastry bag fitted with a ½-inch round tip, divide the batter equally (using even pressure) between the pans, filling about halfway full. Alternatively, you can use a gallon-sized resealable plastic storage bag. Fill the bag and using scissors, remove ½ inch from one of the bottom corners and proceed filling the pans as described above.

3 Bake for 10 to 12 minutes, until the doughnuts spring back when lightly touched. Remove from the oven, invert the doughnuts onto a rack, and allow to cool completely.

4 Make the glaze. In a medium bowl, combine the powdered sugar and water with a whisk, mixing until smooth.

5 Glaze the doughnuts. Dip the top of each doughnut into the glaze and lift, allowing the excess to drip back into the bowl. While the glaze is wet, evenly distribute the coconut on top of the doughnuts. Place the doughnuts on a platter and serve. These doughnuts are best served fresh.

Maple and Bacon
Doughnuts

MAKES 16 LARGE OR 64 MINI DOUGHNUTS

Sweet and savory flavor combinations are very popular today. These doughnuts are a perfect marriage of the two. Try experimenting with different types of bacon such as applewood smoked, maple, or turkey bacon. These are a healthier doughnut because they are baked instead of fried, but you will need either a standard-size doughnut pan or a standard-size mini doughnut pan for baking these.

1   Preheat the oven to 375°F and position an oven rack in the center. Lightly coat the doughnut pans with nonstick cooking spray.

2   Make the doughnuts. In a large bowl, combine the flour, granulated sugar, baking powder, and baking soda with a whisk. Melt the butter in a small pot over low heat and set aside. In a medium bowl, combine the melted butter, buttermilk, eggs, maple syrup, and maple extract with a whisk until foamy, 1 to 2 minutes. Pour the egg mixture into the flour mixture and stir, using a large wooden spoon, until completely combined. Using a pastry bag fitted with a ½-inch round tip, divide the batter equally (using even pressure) between the pans, filling about halfway full. Alternatively, you can use a gallon-sized resealable plastic storage bag. Fill the bag and using scissors, remove ½ inch from one of the bottom corners and proceed filling the pans as described above.

Doughnuts

3 cups unbleached all-purpose flour

1 cup granulated sugar

2 teaspoons baking powder

1 teaspoon baking soda

½ cup (1 stick) salted butter

1 cup buttermilk

3 large eggs, beaten

2 tablespoons maple syrup

1 teaspoon maple extract

Glaze

1¼ cups powdered sugar, sifted

½ cup maple syrup

½ teaspoon maple extract

8 slices crisply cooked bacon, crumbled

3 Bake for 8 to 10 minutes, until the doughnuts spring back when lightly touched. Remove from the oven, invert the doughnuts onto a rack, and allow to cool completely.

4 Make the glaze. In a medium bowl, combine the powdered sugar, maple syrup, and maple extract with a whisk, mixing until smooth.

5 Glaze the doughnuts. Dip the top of each doughnut into the glaze and lift, allowing the excess to drip back into the bowl. While the glaze is wet, evenly distribute the bacon on top of the doughnuts. Place the doughnuts on a platter and serve. These doughnuts are best served fresh.

Caramel Apple
Doughnuts

MAKES 12 LARGE OR 48 MINI DOUGHNUTS

Tart shredded apple and homemade caramel sauce blend together to create a doughnut bursting with flavor. Using Granny Smith apples ensures a more tart doughnut, but try using Red Delicious for more sweetness. These are a healthier doughnut because they are baked instead of fried, but you will need either a standard-size doughnut pan or a standard-size mini doughnut pan for baking these.

1 Preheat the oven to 350°F and position an oven rack in the center. Lightly coat the doughnut pans with nonstick cooking spray.

2 Make the doughnuts. In a medium bowl, combine the flour, baking powder, cinnamon, and salt with a whisk. In a large bowl, combine the eggs, sugars, vegetable oil, and vanilla with a whisk, 1 to 2 minutes; set aside.

3 Using the large holes of a box grater shred both apples (with their skin) just to the cores. Place the shredded apples in a medium mesh strainer to drain, pushing with the back of a wooden spoon to remove excess juice; set aside. Pour the egg mixture into the flour mixture and stir, using a large wooden spoon, until combined. Using a rubber spatula, gently fold in the shredded apples until just combined. Do not overmix. Using a pastry bag fitted with a ½-inch round tip, divide the batter

Doughnuts

1¼ cups unbleached all-purpose flour

2 teaspoons baking powder

½ teaspoon cinnamon

¼ teaspoon salt

2 large eggs, beaten

½ cup brown sugar, firmly packed

½ cup granulated sugar

½ cup vegetable oil

2 teaspoons pure vanilla extract

2 Granny Smith apples, shredded

Caramel

3 tablespoons water

1 tablespoon light corn syrup

¾ cup granulated sugar

⅓ cup heavy cream

1 tablespoon salted butter

equally (using even pressure) between the pans, filling about halfway full. Alternatively, you can use a gallon-sized resealable plastic storage bag. Fill the bag and using scissors, remove ½ inch from one of the bottom corners and proceed filling the pans as described.

4   Bake for 10 to 12 minutes, until the doughnuts spring back when lightly touched. Remove from the oven, invert the doughnuts onto a rack, and allow to cool completely.

5   Make the caramel. Put the water and corn syrup in a medium saucepan. Slowly sprinkle the granulated sugar over the water mixture until it is absorbed. It should look like wet sand. Put the cream into a small saucepan over medium heat and heat it just until it begins to boil. Remove from the heat and set aside. Place the pan with the sugar mixture on the stove over medium heat without stirring until the mixture has dissolved and

is boiling and clear. Turn the heat up to high and boil rapidly, swirling the pot occasionally (do not stir) so the sugar cooks evenly. Cook until the caramel turns a deep golden brown or registers 320°F on a candy thermometer. Immediately turn off the heat and slowly add the warm cream, stirring with a wooden spoon. (Be careful here–the mixture will rise dramatically in the pan and sputter, so you should wear an oven mitt on the hand holding the pan.) Add the butter and stir with a wooden spoon to combine completely. If any bits of caramel have hardened, set the pan over very low heat and stir gently until they melt. Set aside until just warm, approximately 30 minutes.

6   Glaze the doughnuts. Dip the top of each doughnut into the caramel and lift, allowing the excess to drip back into the bowl. Place the doughnuts on a platter and serve. These doughnuts are best served fresh.

Lemon Poppy Seed
Doughnuts

MAKES 9 LARGE OR 36 MINI DOUGHNUTS

A classic combination of lemon and poppy seeds in doughnut form, fresh from your oven, every bite bursts with fresh lemon flavor and the nutty crunch of poppy seeds. Fresh orange juice and zest would make a wonderful substitution for the lemon. These are a healthier doughnut because they are baked instead of fried, but you will need either a standard-size doughnut pan or a standard-size mini doughnut pan for baking these.

1. Preheat the oven to 350°F and position an oven rack in the center. Lightly coat the doughnut pans with nonstick cooking spray.

2. Make the batter. Put the shortening, granulated sugar, and lemon zest in the bowl of a stand mixer fitted with the paddle attachment and cream on medium speed for 2 to 3 minutes, until light and fluffy. Scrape the sides of the bowl with a rubber spatula as needed. With the machine running on low speed, add the egg and mix until incorporated.

3. In a medium bowl, combine the flour, baking powder, salt, and poppy seeds with a whisk. With the machine running on low speed, add half the dry ingredients and mix until just combined. Add the milk and mix in, then add the rest of the dry ingredients and mix until just combined. Using a pastry bag fitted with a ½-inch round tip, divide the batter equally

(using even pressure) between the pans, filling approximately halfway full. Alternatively, you can use a gallon-sized resealable plastic storage bag. Fill the bag and using scissors, remove ½ inch from one of the bottom corners and proceed filling the pans as described.

4   Bake for 10 to 12 minutes, until the doughnuts spring back when lightly touched. Remove from the oven, invert the doughnuts onto a rack, and allow to cool completely.

5   Make the glaze. In a medium bowl, combine the powdered sugar and lemon juice with a whisk, mixing until smooth.

6   Glaze the doughnuts. Dip the top of each doughnut into the glaze and lift, allowing the excess to drip back into the bowl. Whisk the glaze from time to time to prevent a crust from forming. Place the doughnuts on a platter and serve. These doughnuts are best served fresh.

Ingredients

Doughnuts

2½ cups unbleached all-purpose flour

1 cup sugar

½ cup unsweetened cocoa powder

2 teaspoons cinnamon

2 teaspoons baking powder

1 teaspoon baking soda

½ cup (1 stick) salted butter

1 cup buttermilk

3 large eggs, beaten

2 tablespoons honey

Glaze

½ cup semisweet chocolate morsels

6 tablespoons (¾ stick) salted butter

¼ teaspoon ground chipotle chile pepper

Spiced Chocolate
Doughnuts

MAKES 16 LARGE OR 64 MINI DOUGHNUTS

Bring a taste of Mexico to a classic chocolate doughnut by adding cinnamon and chipotle pepper. You can adjust the heat by adding or subtracting the chile pepper to your taste. These are a healthier doughnut because they are baked instead of fried, but you will need either a standard-size doughnut pan or a standard-size mini doughnut pan for baking these.

1 Preheat the oven to 375°F and position an oven rack in the center. Lightly coat the doughnut pans with nonstick cooking spray.

2 Make the doughnuts. In a large bowl, combine the flour, sugar, cocoa powder, cinnamon, baking powder, and baking soda with a whisk. Melt the butter in a small pot over low heat and set aside. In a medium bowl, combine the melted butter, buttermilk, eggs, and honey with a whisk until foamy, 1 to 2 minutes. Pour the egg mixture into the flour mixture and stir, using a large wooden spoon, until completely combined. Using a pastry bag fitted with a ½-inch round tip, divide the batter equally (using even pressure) between the pans, filling about halfway full. Alternatively, you can use a gallon-sized resealable plastic storage bag. Fill the bag and using scissors, remove ½ inch from one of the bottom corners and proceed filling the pans as described above.

3 Bake for 8 to 10 minutes, until the doughnuts spring back when lightly touched. Remove from the oven, invert the doughnuts onto a rack, and allow to cool completely.

4 Make the glaze. Place the chocolate morsels in a medium heatproof bowl and place over a small pot of simmering water, being sure the bowl is not touching the water. Turn off the burner and allow the chocolate to melt completely, occasionally stirring with a heatproof rubber spatula. Stir in the butter until completely melted and combined, then add the chipotle chile pepper and stir to combine. Remove the bowl from the pot and set aside.

5 Glaze the doughnuts. Dip the top of each doughnut into the glaze and lift, allowing the excess to drip back into the bowl. The glaze will harden slightly as it cools. Place the doughnuts on a platter and serve. These doughnuts are best served fresh.

Metric Conversions and Equivalents

Metric Conversion Formulas

TO CONVERT	MULTIPLY
Ounces to grams	Ounces by 28.35
Pounds to kilograms	Pounds by .454
Teaspoons to milliliters	Teaspoons by 4.93
Tablespoons to milliliters	Tablespoons by 14.79
Fluid ounces to milliliters	Fluid ounces by 29.57
Cups to milliliters	Cups by 236.59
Cups to liters	Cups by .236
Pints to liters	Pints by .473
Quarts to liters	Quarts by .946
Gallons to liters	Gallons by 3.785
Inches to centimeters	Inches by 2.54

Approximate Metric Equivalents

VOLUME

¼ teaspoon	1 milliliter
½ teaspoon	2.5 milliliters
¾ teaspoon	4 milliliters
1 teaspoon	5 milliliters
2 teaspoons	10 milliliters
1 tablespoon (½ fluid ounce)	15 milliliters
¼ cup	60 milliliters
⅓ cup	80 milliliters
½ cup (4 fluid ounces)	120 milliliters
⅔ cup	160 milliliters
¾ cup	180 milliliters
1 cup (8 fluid ounces)	240 milliliters
2 cups (1 pint)	460 milliliters
3 cups	700 milliliters
4 cups (1 quart)	.95 liter
1 quart plus ¼ cup	1 liter
4 quarts (1 gallon)	3.8 liters

WEIGHT

¼ ounce	7 grams
½ ounce	14 grams
¾ ounce	21 grams
1 ounce	28 grams
2 ounces	57 grams
3 ounces	85 grams
4 ounces (¼ pound)	113 grams
5 ounces	142 grams
6 ounces	170 grams
7 ounces	198 grams
8 ounces (½ pound)	227 grams
16 ounces (1 pound)	454 grams
35.25 ounces (2.2 pounds)	1 kilogram

LENGTH

¼ inch	6 millimeters
½ inch	1¼ centimeters
1 inch	2½ centimeters
2 inches	5 centimeters
6 inches	15¼ centimeters
12 inches (1 foot)	30 centimeters

Oven Temperatures
To convert Fahrenheit to Celsius, subtract 32 from Fahrenheit, multiply the result by 5, then divide by 9.

Description	Fahrenheit	Celsius	British Gas Mark
Very cool	200°	95°	0
Very cool	225°	110°	¼
Very cool	250°	120°	½
Cool	275°	135°	1
Cool	300°	150°	2
Warm	325°	165°	3
Moderate	350°	175°	4
Moderately hot	375°	190°	5
Fairly hot	400°	200°	6
Hot	425°	220°	7
Very hot	450°	230°	8
Very hot	475°	245°	9

Common Ingredients and Their Approximate Equivalents
1 cup uncooked rice = 225 grams
1 cup all-purpose flour = 140 grams
1 stick butter (4 ounces • ½ cup • 8 tablespoons) = 110 grams
1 cup butter (8 ounces • 2 sticks • 16 tablespoons) = 220 grams
1 cup brown sugar, firmly packed = 225 grams
1 cup granulated sugar = 200 grams

Information compiled from *Recipes into Type* by Joan Whitman and Dolores Simon (Newton, MA: Biscuit Books, 2000); *The New Food Lover's Companion* by Sharon Tyler Herbst (Hauppauge, NY: Barron's, 1995); and *Rosemary Brown's Big Kitchen Instruction Book* (Kansas City, MO: Andrews McMeel, 1998).

Acknowledgments

What makes *So Sweet!* so sweet are the folks that brought it to life. Thanks to Jean Lucas and Kirsty Melville for their support of the concept, as well as Tim Lynch and Julie Barnes at Andrews McMeel for their artistic vision. Cindy Mushet, Paul Rocque, and Diane Mora made the book smile with their tasty recipes, and Ben Pieper and the JohnsonRauhoff photography teams brought the recipes to life on the pages of the book. Ben was ably assisted by Dan Trefz and Max Wagner. At JohnsonRauhoff, Elizabeth Kohler and Rob Regovich, Ashley Ampersee, Pete Strzyzykowski, Lyn Wilson, and Paige Zars were a well-oiled machine. Without the support and tenacity of Bryan Habeck, Felicia Chao, Mark Beard, Tony Dellino, Morgan McQuade, and Gregory Chandler from Sur La Table, the book would just be a dream. And for making us smile, kudos to Jack Lucas. But thanks most of all to our customers, whose delight in all things sweet make every day at Sur La Table *so sweet*!!

Index